NEVER GIVE UP!

Life Through A Song

ANGELA MARTINEZ

ISBN 978-1-7341486-0-2

Front and back cover designed by: Kyro Wolf

Photography for back of book: by David Bean

Printed in the United States of America

First Printing, 2019

This book is dedicated to my precious little miracle. Isabella my sweet daughter, you are my heart, my inspiration, my joy, and my reason for everything that I do.

CONTENTS

Introduction

I am sure all of us can think back to a moment where a song has played a part in memorializing a moment that we will never forget. Music is always there in the background to take us back to that moment. When we hear it, it's almost like magic. All of the feelings and emotions come flooding back, good and bad, just as if we are living in that moment all over again.

This book "Never Give Up" is about facing life head on no matter what we are faced with and overcoming every obstacle in our way and at the same time learning to become a stronger, kinder, fulfilled, and more empowered human being and learning life's lessons along the way.

As far back as I can remember music has always been in my life. The story goes that mom used to take me back and forth to day care, and as she drove she would sing to me. One night before I was able to talk she had the baby monitor on while I was lying in my crib. She heard me humming the melody of one of the songs she often would sing to me and she said she knew right away that singing was going to be an important part of my life. I learned very early on how powerful music is and the impact it can have on people.

My life has been made up of a collection of moments that always seemed to be intertwined with a song. All of the songs that I can think of one by one, as I reflect on them have gotten me to where I am today. It's through that emotion and inspiration from music and life that I was able to co-write with Shelly Riff the song "Never Give Up." The song "Never Give Up" is very special to me. It has touched me in a different way than any song I have ever been a part of. I guess maybe it's the concept and the topic and the way the opportunity to write it presented itself that evokes that feeling. It has made me look at music differently than I ever have before. It made me realize how music is woven into every single facet of my life from my heart wrenching heart breaks, to the scariest experiences, to my most happiest and cherished moments. Music was always there to pick me back up and guide me through.

Music has always been a part of my journey and such an intricate part of who I am. Certain songs at certain times have signified very important moments in my life. One in particular is a song I wrote called "Right There." It helped me bring awareness to a disease called Scleroderma. The lyric, "if you go looking for the truth the answer will be right there," has spoken volumes to many patients fighting to survive this chronic autoimmune condition. The experience of sharing the music helped me understand the true power of a song. Another is the one that started the beginning of my professional music career when I was 14 years old, a song I co-wrote with music producer Slammin' Sam called "My Heart is Here." The lyrics "my heart is here don't take away my love my soul. It's right here can't you see, the one to hold." I was so young but my ability to deliver passion was able to transcend my age which allowed me to inspire people of all ages. I have been called an old soul all of my life. And singing was my way to tell the story of what was in my heart.

We all have a never give up story inside each and every one of us. We all go through difficult moments that shape us into who we are. Through these pages you will learn about my life and the obstacles that I have encountered, and the life stories of other people who have had never give up moments in their lives and how they overcame them with knowledge, strength, and perseverance. You will see the warriors that we have all become as we faced life's biggest challenges and how we overcame them by never giving up and finding our warrior within.

I hope as you read these stories you realize that you are not alone. We are all in this together. This book is for anyone who has had a struggle in their life that they needed to overcome, had a challenging situation to push through, or are maybe still in that tough place in their life where they need encouragement. If that sounds like you, let "Never Give Up" be your anthem and let this book be your guide.

Chapter 1

Every Day Is a New Beginning

We all breathe in and out, close our eyes, and at one point fall asleep. Then we open our eyes again to experience the beauty that the world has to offer. It's the same for every one of us.

We all get into a routine. We wake up, brush our teeth, take a shower, brush our hair, put on clothes, eat breakfast, and begin our day. This becomes familiar to us, and it feels comfortable. But then one day something happens, and the familiarity that we know so well changes. Waking up and opening our eyes, looking around everything feels foreign, strange, and completely different. And it changes you in ways you never even imagined.

It might be when you wake up early, open your eyes, and go to your new job, you are now the boss. And it requires more time than a regular job ever did. It might be when you have conquered those twelve grueling steps, those awful hangovers you once had over and over are something you will never feel again. You may wake up and hear that due to a horrific accident you will never take a step again, but the diagnosis doesn't work for you—so you find a way to defy the odds.

You see your best friend and life partner going through one of his or her scariest moments in life and all you want to do is take the fear and pain away. Maybe you're looking at a medication bottle where every pill you take is one step closer to living a longer life, or just the opposite, and you realize that throwing those pills away means no more pain. Maybe you wake up and travel from hospital to hospital to brighten the lives of young children fighting to take their last breaths or cheat death by fighting for your own life when coming face to face with a gun. For me it's singing a song that comes straight from my heart, knowing once the world hears it, it will be forever changed.

We all have moments that change everything.

You can open your eyes in the morning and go for a walk, being blinded by the bright sunshine and breathing in the cool crisp air, and then the next, be faced with a completely different reality.

The freedom you once knew is gone and has been replaced by a small cell and iron bars filled with dim light and a chill that never seems to go away. You have a knowing deep inside that your life will never be the same. We often imprison ourselves through our thoughts and our insecurities which keep us captive from our dreams. But once we realize we hold the key to our own success then we will never give up.

"No matter how hard the past has been you can always begin again"

-Buddha

Life story by Inmate #94242-111

The heavy mechanical door to my cell slides open, waking me up from a dream—a dream of having family, of having a home, a dream of escaping poverty. I am also waking up realizing that what I did was wrong.

Selling drugs is a "victimless" crime—if you don't consider the children of the addicts or any of their loved ones. It's victimless if you don't consider the community. Despite what your favorite rapper says, there was no glamour to my drug sales. There were however, snakes, snitches, death, and deceit. Drugs bring out the worst in even the most beautiful people. I, myself, became uglier just by selling them. I became arrogant, vain, and unforgiving. I became heartless.

When I was growing up, both my parents were addicted to drugs. They tried to sell crank to support their habit. My dad killed himself when I was fourteen. By then, I was already trying to sell crack on my own. My first nights out, I was scared, intimidated, and totally unsure of myself. My mom selling crank to her friends at home was a world different than me selling rocks on the street at night. It seemed like the addicts knew every trick in the book to swindle me out of what little I had. When that didn't work, they simply beat me up and robbed me. I was embarrassed, but nights spent starving with my little sister pushed me into determination. Summer days were spent on the block, burning up. I was still out there on cold winter nights, bundled up.

My first days in prison were extremely difficult. I had experienced some terrible things in life, but this was the worst. I was so depressed, missing my family, I couldn't even function. I constantly thought about killing myself. Days, months, and years went by, with me dwelling on the past. I couldn't believe I had been sentenced so long for such a petty offense. Today, that past is all behind me. Today is a different day. Today, I move forward.

I'm still in prison, still immersed in a life of gangs, drugs, and violence. Temptation is still omnipresent, disguised as solutions to my everyday problems. I'm still striving for a better life, and I'm still laughed at when I try.

Everyday is the same, yet completely different. I want no part of the gangs, drugs, and violence that I'm so deeply rooted in. I'm stronger than the temptation that suffocates my pride. And I now know there is a better life, and I am capable of it.

I still get laughed at. It's for different reasons now. It's no longer because my only pair of jeans was somebody's ripped-up, dirty hand-me-downs. It's no longer because my shoes came from the Salvation Army. I still can't fit in. But it's no longer because I switched schools every time we went homeless. I get laughed at, but now it's because I'm in prison.

I was taken from my family, thrown in jail, and sentenced to twenty-seven years in prison for a petty, nonviolent drug sale. I have been here for eleven years. Since then, my mom has died, my wife has divorced me, and I haven't seen my daughter in years, but I won't let this get me down. I've been jumped, beat up, and stabbed numerous times. I have always had to fight. I've battled depression and had to accept the fact that I don't mean anything to anybody. I have tripped, stumbled, and fallen over and over again. I continue to get back up, dust myself off. I will not let prison ruin my life. I won't let where I'm at dictate where I want to go. I won't be a victim of my circumstances. I won't even consider my circumstances. I didn't come to prison to grow weak, to give up on my dream. I'm not here to give up.

I'm trying to go to school and take classes for job skills instead of hanging out with my gang. Everything has changed in my life.

Homies no longer look up to me, but resent me. They probably laugh and talk behind my back. I don't care. I got to know a better life. A life of family night, of church, and of eating dinner at a table—all things I had never experienced before. I got to know a life of being called, "Dad," "Babe," and "Son." I had the most beautiful in-laws one can have. I've also come to know a life of finally being able to be a good son for my mom. This is the life I got to know; and that life is gone now.

If I'm going to get this life back, it's going to take work, hard work, and dedication—work on myself as well as my future. No more wasting time in here by drinking, gambling, and watching TV. No more making connections for the wrong reasons. I can't fall into the trap of prison life, becoming deeper involved in my gang, or relieve my insecurities by seeking companionship with outside women. No more moping around, feeling sorry for myself.

Now is the time to be strong. Now I have to be disciplined. It's not easy going to school, and it's not easy keeping up with the work, but it's something I have to do. I'm not even sure I can get a job when I do get out. I know I can get meth, but a job, I'm not sure of. I've never had a job in my life. I don't know where to start. Even if I can get one, I'm not even sure it'll be good enough to support me and cover my responsibilities as a dad. I'm a man in my thirties, and I'll be starting at the bottom. It's going to take a lot of humility, a lot of struggle—all for a life I probably can't even have back. My wife has left me, and my daughter never writes back. This has been really hard for me. It took a strength I didn't know I had. I can't give up, though. I have to be strong. I have to try. I have to give it my all.

Those days are behind me now. That life is too. Now, if I'm going to make my life a success, I will need that same drive and determination I had then. What's crazy is the real challenge hasn't even started yet. That happens when I get out. It's important that I prepare myself now, that I better myself now because I will never give up.

Every Day Is a New Beginning

Chapter 2

Fear

Fear. This word couldn't have been more true for me in 2003. I had just turned nineteen and I had been traveling back and forth from California to Nashville. Life was about to take a turn and this was about to be the biggest decision my family and I have ever made. I had just graduated from Los Medanos College in Pittsburg, CA with an Associate in Arts (AA) degree in liberal arts. I could have just transferred to a four-year college, but I told myself, if I'm going to go to school all that time, I better have something to show for it. So I walked with my graduating class, got my associate degree, and then Nashville came calling.

After I had flown from California to Tennessee about nine times due to music, Mom and I tried to convince my Dad that moving to Nashville was the best thing for my career. It took us a while, but one day we found out that Dad was getting laid off. He uttered the magical words, "let's go to Nashville." and the next thing he knew there was a for-sale sign in our yard. Two days later, the house had a sold sign, and shortly after we loaded up a moving truck and were headed on our three-day drive to move to the country music capital of the world: Nashville, Tennessee. And everything was going to change.

Now we did something that I recommend you never do and that's buying your house off the internet. But you live and you learn. It's pretty crazy, I know. Mom went to the closing, but Dad and I had not seen the house until we got to the driveway. And the word "driveway" was an understatement. It was more like a tiny mountain at a ninety-degree angle. As we drove up, we felt like we needed the emergency brake just to keep from sliding back down. When it snowed, we actually did slide down! Which is even scarier than it sounds. Mainly because when we were sliding down we had no control what so ever. We missed a car by a hair. And that was the first and last time I parked in the driveway during winter time.

The house itself was nice, but my neighbor turned out to be pretty much living in my backyard, a stone's throw away. This was a total shock, since the realtor who had sent the pics made it seem like we had our own private paradise. Pictures can be deceiving. Just look at social media. I will say though that the neighbors ended up being pretty cool. The guy on the right behind us was one of the writers on the song "Ol' Red" for Blake Shelton and the other neighbor was an awesome costume designer for the Opry stars.

I had never lived anywhere but California. All of the people I had known, the places where I had experienced life and the memories that I'd made had all been left in the California dust. (2,275.6 miles of dust to be exact.) I can remember feeling fearful as I looked around at an unfamiliar territory of wide-open spaces, no fences in sight, and traffic lights that looked like they would wobble and fly right off the line if the wind got angry enough. The security and comfort of seeing familiar smiling faces at the store or the mall was a thing of the past. And reality set in: I had done it. I was now in the place where I could follow my dreams, and I knew at that moment that I would never give up, no matter what. Fear was there but it wasn't going to overtake me. Love, passion, and determination were and I had to believe in myself and my dreams and realize that I could do anything I set my heart to. And you can too. It may seem scary and out of reach but that is the moment when you have to give it your all. There is a saying that became popular. YOLO, You only live once. But that's not true. You only die once. You live every day. So it's up to you make every minute worth living for.

"Limits, like fears, are often just an illusion"

-Michael Jordan

Life story by Mignon Francois, Owner and Founder of the Cupcake Collection

I'm Mignon Francois from New Orleans, Louisiana. A mother of what I call six plus one. I raised six children, and then halfway through that, one attached herself to us, so I finished raising her. I have been living in Nashville, Tennessee, since 2003 in an area called Germantown, which at the time really didn't have much name recognition. (We take a lot of pride in what has happened to Germantown, and we feel partly responsible for it becoming a little "it" town in this little "it" city.)

Before we opened the Cupcake Collection, there had never been anything like it in this area. It was really thinking outside the box to bring this sort of shop to the neighborhood. It was divine intervention, almost like Immaculate Conception; how God just let it plant into my spirit that I could open a bakery and have a bake sale every day to save my family from the debt and brokenness we were living in.

We didn't have enough money, enough resources, and many days, we lived in the home that the bakery is housed in without light or running water because we couldn't pay the bills. When I got it in my spirit that this is what I was supposed to, I started moving every day. I had no knowledge of business. I had no money, and I had no credit—all of the things you're supposed to have for a successful business. But I believed that there was nothing I had to lose.

I figured cupcakes weren't a thing in Nashville yet and I

thought it was going to be simpler than it was. I didn't know how hard it was to decorate them and make them look pretty. In the beginning I started calling the city and getting all the rules and things I needed. Just the supplies overtook this room, and there'd be no room to do anything else. We had another room in our house that was pretty much unused, except for my then husband. We had looked around for a space, but we just couldn't afford anything. He said, "If you stick with this idea, I'll give you my man cave." So that's where the bakery was born. I think it's funny that cupcakes are sold out of a former man cave.

A lot of people think that it's supposed to happen really fast, and that's why they give up on things. It took me two years working at this business every day like it was a job for this store to open. Once you become successful at something, you realize it's like you broke the ceiling. While you're going through it, it feels so hard. But when you do it and finish, you're like, "That really was kind of easy. And now I can do it again and again."

I also realized that when things come to you, you have to execute them now. I've been trying to teach this concept to people about "now faith." There's a Bible verse that says, "Now faith is a substance of things hoped for, the evidence of things not seen." If you could just unlock the sentence and understand where the comma falls, it lets you know that the words "now" and "faith" go together. The "now" is describing faith. People mix that Bible verse up. They just think that's what faith is; a substance of things hoped for, the evidence of things not seen. That's not true. Faith is simply believing in something that hasn't been proven. There are different levels and varieties of faith. "Now faith" is the thing that makes things happen. When you get an idea, or when something comes into your heart, you get up and start moving now on it. Faith that makes God do things on your behalf, that activates the power of God, is called "now faith." And that's the kind of faith that will let you open a business when you don't even know how to bake.

We can do anything. I said everything spiritually, but if you want to think about it scientifically we don't use but a portion of our brain. I think about David Blaine, the magician, and how he makes things move or levitate. How do you do that? It's mind over matter, and he's not willing to give up until he gets the answer. It's like Dorothy in the movie The Wizard of Oz. You always had the *answer. It was inside of you—that gut feeling that's right up underneath your rib cage, that's where butterflies live. That's where you hear God speak to you. It's not really butterflies. It's anxiousness to actually follow through with something. It's also that place when you really want to go ask a question, but you're scared.*

We allow fear to block us from doing things that we need to do. We second-guess ourselves, and we count our own selves out. He's the giver of all good things. And there's a Bible verse that says, "If you then who are evil, know how to give good gifts to your children, how much more will your Father who is in heaven give good things to those who ask him!" When I found out that I was good enough; and started working for me and valuing me, I had all these ideas inside of me. I wasn't a scatterbrain. I had a gift called ideation. When I started getting that in my spirit and started grinding for myself I was not willing to give up on myself anymore. This is the time that the business grew.

When I think of the idea of never give up, I think about a surprise party—how people are waiting in the dark to surprise you when you walk in and turn on the lights. But if you never go through that door—and instead you say, "I made it all this way, but you know what? I'm going home." And you leave. You left the party and went home before you ever opened the door and realized all these people were waiting there to celebrate you. That's what we do to ourselves in life. We give up right before it's time to go into the party. If you only knew if you just walked through that door everything in your life was about to change.

I remember back when it was a cool thing to get forwards on e-mails, and people were forwarding stories around. And there was a story that talks about a man who died and went to heaven. He's walking around heaven with an angel, and the angel would never let him go in a particular room that was closed. The man was like, "Why won't you ever let me go in that room?" And the angel replied, "You can't handle what's in that room." He said, "If you want to go in there, you can; I just want you to know you can't handle what's in that room." So, because of the man's curiosity, he goes inside the room, and there are all these boxes in there with his name on them. The guy says to the angel, "Why do all these packages have my name on them?" The angel replies, "Those were all the things God wanted to give you, but you never asked." How many things are we missing out on because we give up too soon? We don't ask for help, and we don't ask God.

God dreams a bigger dream for you than you dream for yourself.

I heard the author Shaunna Barbee say, "Fear is not our gift." Of all the things that God has given you, fear is not one of the things he gave you. If you use your mind just a little bit more than average, you can be successful. The only difference between me and someone else that's not doing it is my focus on never giving up. That's what made me successful. The only difference between me and the person who says they want to have a successful bakery is that I wouldn't quit, and they do, every day. It's the only thing that makes us different.

"Everything I want to do I want it to glorify God because I know that only what I do for Christ will last. I expect this business to live for Christ, and I expect it to be around a really long time."

Now we have grown. We have other locations of our store. We've had a mobile store, traveled with our cupcakes, and done pop-up shops in other cities. We also have a scholarship in our name. This is about so much more than cupcakes. Now I've been going back into the community and seeing other people doing business, and when I think they're doing business well I offer advice and give them the opportunity to sit and talk and they grow.

I remember when I first heard the quote by Melba Colgrove. "Joy is the feeling of grinning on the inside." It made me feel so happy! I want to make sure that when people come into my business they experience joy on the inside.

The Cupcake Collection has received many awards since its opening in 2008. It has appeared on ABC's The Chew, in the Among the Beautiful series, honored as the best cupcakes in the United States at thrillist.com, named

as one of the fifty things to eat in Nashville before you die, awarded as one of the top food trucks in Nashville, Named as one of the best desserts in Nashville. It also gives back and has been recognized for selling cupcakes to benefit children's cancer research and partnering with the Second Harvest Food Bank. And one of Francois's proudest accomplishments is getting a college scholarship in her name.

To find out more about the cupcake collection go to:

https://www.thecupcakecollection.com/

Fear

Chapter 3

Love the Addict; Hate the Addiction

Addiction is defined by dictionary.com as the state of being enslaved to a habit or practice, or to something that is psychologically or physically habit-forming, such as narcotics, to such an extent that its cessation causes severe trauma.

I think all of us are addicted to something in one way or another, even if we don't want to admit it. Some people are addicted to food. Some people are addicted to drugs, alcohol, and some are even addicted to sex. There are so many addictions that are out there. Me, I was addicted to love which made for a lot of great songs and bad relationships. Not to be confused with a sex addict. A love addict is a person that is in love with the idea of being in love. And the initial feelings of euphoria and happiness they feel in the beginning with their partner is what keeps them in a bad relationship for far too long.

I had followed that same road for a long time. I didn't know it then, but as I look back on the pattern of how my relationships were, it was always the same. It was like I was dating the same man. He just had a different name, age, and phone number. But the characteristics were always the same. He was good-looking, outgoing, athletic, and smart. The worst part was he knew how to get to my heart, knowing my deepest insecurities and fears and using them to manipulate me. He would isolate me from my friends and family and only said and did good things when it was convenient for him. He would also prey on my never ending desire to find love. When I felt love it was like a high you can't even explain. The world seemed brighter, the birds sang more beautifully and I literally felt like I was glowing. I had a smile that wouldn't fade and although they tried no one could tell me anything negative about that person. My heart wouldn't allow it.

I was addicted to every part of what love was supposed to be. And along with that addiction to love, came pain because this type of love wasn't based on something real. It was fast, with a whirlwind of passionate promises and romance. These men knew what I wanted and how to bring my fantasy to life. They knew what to say and how to say it to feed my addiction and keep me wanting more. It was great in the beginning but it never stayed that way. I can't say that I craved being hurt, because I know for a fact that I hated that. The big ugly cries and nights of sitting alone with my pillow were not my idea of a good time. But what I was addicted to and what I craved was the way they made me feel after they hurt me. These guys behaved like prince charming when they were trying to make me happy and then again when they tried to make up for the hurtful things they said or did. They were experts at that. Their words would roll off their tongues like butter. I could almost drown in them. They just overwhelmed my soul, and I would get lost in the sentiment and passion, even if deep down, I knew at some level they were lies.

Instead of just a simple "I'm sorry," and moving on, like most guys, they would apologize in sweet and heartfelt ways with roses, letters, dedications of songs on the radio, expensive dates, moving across the country and the most romantic proposals you could think of. He'd do anything that tricked my heart back into having faith in him again. The hardest and most confusing part for me was after the big, grandiose apology. He wouldn't mess up right away. He would behave like the type of man any woman dreams about. But then, after months on end of being what I wanted him to be he would slip back to the behaviors that he knew so well, and we would be back at square one all over again.

I guess the part that was so addicting about a relationship was that I didn't know what was going to happen next. It was like being on a new roller coaster that I had no control over and every turn was a surprise. I craved that feeling of not knowing and the spontaneity it created, since I wouldn't allow it in any other part of my life. There were romantic twists and turns and then sudden heartbreaking drops and my emotions would go from zero to sixty. But eventually it would become nothing but drops, and I would lose myself in the pain. It took one long relationship like this for me to see what was truly happening before I was able to get off that crazy ride. It took me from my weakest moment to having to be the strongest I had ever been. I had to literally pick myself up off the floor and stand up and say enough was enough.

I believe the key to success is knowing why things happen. In my life I like having control over things. I can admit that. I don't really make any move in my life until it has been planned, looked at from every angle, and analyzed completely to death—so there's no way that it can possibly go wrong, at least by my calculations. But relationships are different. I have seen my parents and the way they interact and love each other, and control is no part of that. It works because two people, who are completely free to do whatever they want, choose to do what they do because of their unconditional love for their partner. Love is very freeing.

I am a commitment girl. That has been ingrained in me since I was little, and that's just part of who I am. My dad taught me that when you commit to something you follow it through. I can remember as a kid that I had committed to singing at church for an event that was coming up weeks later. Well, that same weekend, my friends invited me to go to Marine World, now called Six Flags Discovery Kingdom. I asked my dad, and he said, "Absolutely not. You made a commitment to sing at the church, and that's what you are going to do." So I have lived by that rule in all aspects of my life. It is great in business, but not always in relationships. When a relationship headed in the wrong direction, instead of walking away I would hold on until there was nothing left. That was almost easier than going through the pain of losing the relationship. This kept me in relationships much longer than I should have been. I would never give up even when I should have.

I have now come to a point in my life where I realize that's what was happening. I think discovering that is the biggest success of all. Realizing I had a problem, I can now see it for what it really was. And also realizing too, that I was strong enough to overcome it. I have learned that I don't have to make a relationship work if it's not working. I can just let it go. Just because you are in a relationship with someone it doesn't mean that you are meant to be together and it has to work. Sometimes it just doesn't, no matter what you do or say. It doesn't make either person bad or wrong—it just wasn't meant to be. And you move on and go down the road that God has planned for you. And at the right time and place you will find your soul mate.

This was the toughest lesson I had ever learned but also the best. By the time that five year relationship was over I had been broken in every way possible. The anxiety that was created from being wanted, and then unwanted over and over again was exhausting and I was done with it. And I felt the best thing to do was to let it go. I chose to end it that day and never look back. It is hard but I have learned not to carry that anger with me and to forgive him. Not just for him, but for me. I no longer carry that burden and I wish him happiness and love.

God has a person for each of us and when it doesn't work it just means that person wasn't God's choice for you. And there's someone else out there that's better suited for you. Despite my failed relationships and broken hearts, I have learned through it all how strong I truly am. What I thought would break me instead showed me that I am unbreakable. What I thought would destroy me instead gave me a new sense of creativity and helped shape who I am today. What I thought would scare me instead brought out the bravery and warrior that was there all along. And despite everything I went through, when it comes to relationships, I will never give up on love.

"Life begins when addiction ends"

-unknown

Life story by Karen Mock

Lies had become a way of life with me. There were lies woven into everything I did. I had a million excuses at the ready when I let someone down or failed to achieve a goal. It was basic survival instinct. And, after a while, I had to have alcohol in my blood to feel normal. I couldn't live sober anymore. Feeding the emptiness in my soul became my priority. I felt empowered, more confident, and able to conquer the world with a few drinks in me.

I was leading a double life. I was always rushing around, trying to get everything done that everyone expected me to get done and still have plenty of time to feed my addiction. I had to work in the time to get to feeling the way I wanted to so I could carry on with my day. There is no other word to describe this activity except insanity—the insanity of alcoholism. I eventually caught up with myself! I became the lies.

I had totally lost my reasoning ability to determine right from wrong. Oh, I knew what was right. I just convinced myself that I had to do wrong things. And when I did, I had to fix the mistakes with another drink and another lie. It was a frightening way to live—always being on the edge of a cliff, waiting to fall off and end the whole façade that was my life. I had condemned myself to prison. My mind was held captive by my inability to stop drinking. I always managed to convince myself that if I could just stay drunk, the world around me would keep functioning just fine without my participation. Of course, I was wrong again. I made the wrong decisions again; I got the same consequences again. Insanity was my reality!

I worked in high-tech advertising agencies for many years. I was fortunate enough to be in the right place at the right time to get my career on track. I had always studied and analyzed advertisements. It was a hobby of mine. God was gracious enough to give me the miracle of success, and I had a great run. I was good at creating advertising campaigns, and my husband is an engineer, so he tutored me on why a certain technical innovation might or might not be the next hot widget. I advanced to vice-president of new business development in a couple of years. This position required a lot of entertaining—I wined and dined hundreds of new clients over the years. What a perfect job for a blooming alcoholic!

Then, I was in a serious car accident and broke my face in several places. My jaw was shattered. I had several corrective surgeries over the course of a couple of years. I had an implant put in for a jawbone and went through therapy to learn how to make my new jaw move properly. During this time, I was prescribed some strong pain medications. I took them. Pretty soon, I started taking them with beer instead of water, and they made me feel really happy and okay with my deformities. Deformities! Again, by the grace of God, my face had not been permanently disfigured. Now I look pretty good for an old woman. But that experience then took such an emotional toll on me that I had to drink to function normally in my work and in my home life. So, at this point in time, I began to exhibit my genetic alcoholic behavior.

Alcoholism runs rampant in my family. I should have known to be very afraid of alcohol, but, I just ran with the good feelings and denied that I had a drinking problem. I started my downhill run into full-blown alcoholic behavior. I drank moderately in front of people and then would finish getting pass-out blotto when I was alone. I hid when and how much I drank.

The lies started being a way of life for me. I had to cover up my problem with them. I tried a couple of times during this time to go to AA but failed miserably. I would drink on the way to the meetings and on the way home. That's insanity at its finest. I went to appease my family and friends, as they believed I was endangering my very existence with the drinking. I couldn't hear them. I didn't want to hear them. I ignored them.

I got so bad, it was impossible for my husband to put up with me anymore. I was slowly killing myself right in front of him, and he couldn't stop me. He finally left. So, there I was on my couch, looking out my front window, watching him drive away. I felt betrayed, afraid, and relieved in a way that he had left me to my own demise. By the time he left, I was so sick with alcohol poisoning I could barely get up off that couch. I had two dogs at the time that I needed to take care of. It was all I could do physically to feed them and let them outside a few times a day. They were my only companions. They laid around with me and looked sad and confused, wondering what was wrong with their mommy.

I had pretty much decided that my life was over. My skin was bright yellow and my stomach extended to the point that I looked pregnant. I had zero energy and zero appetite, and drinking just made me sicker. Alcohol stopped making things better. I didn't even think about going to the doctor. I knew I couldn't get treatment, because I had no health insurance and couldn't pay for a doctor's visit, much less a hospital stay. I knew the hospital would not admit me under these circumstances, so out of shame, I just sat there and tried to die. I couldn't even get that right! I had given up all hope. I prayed for God to take me with him or make me well. I was done with it all. I couldn't go on like I was.

I was at the point where I had to change my path in life or die. If I didn't die, I was going to get myself put in jail for drunk driving or vehicular homicide, or the men in the white coats were going to come and lock me away in a mental institution. I needed a miracle.

Then, lo and behold, I looked out my window one morning, and there was a strange car in my driveway. Of course, I had no idea who was driving it. When the woman got out and started walking up to my door, I saw that it was Sheila, my oldest daughter.

She knocked on my door, but I was hesitant to open it. I was ashamed of how I looked and how the house looked, and I didn't want to let her see what a mess I was. Even when I knew it was her, I was in shock. She lived all the way out in California, and I was in Illinois. Could she really be here? For a minute, I thought I was hallucinating. I had not spoken to anyone in my family for weeks. The phone had been cut off by this time, and I had no electricity to run a computer or e-mail or anything. I was isolated. My three daughters had sensed that something was seriously wrong.

I had ignored several important events. A grandbaby had been born, and I didn't call. I didn't speak to my oldest grandchild on her birthday. I just pretended that no one cared anymore and that no one would notice that I had become a stranger to them all. How could I have dismissed them like that? I was mentally preparing myself to be nothing anymore. They would all be better off if I just died.

Sheila was the one elected by the kids to come and check on me. Her husband hadn't wanted her to come, as he had feared she would find me dead. I was blessed with a moment of clarity that day. I knew that God had sent her to help me. He had answered my prayer! My real-life guardian angel had been sent to me to save my life. I know that without God and Sheila's intervention, I would not be writing this, 'cause I would be dead.

I had been saved again! Sheila cleaned me up as best she could. I hadn't had a shower for quite a while. I was too weak to wash myself, so she did it for me. She found some decent clothes, dressed me, and dragged me fighting to her car and took me to the hospital. I kept telling her, they wouldn't keep me because I couldn't pay. She said emphatically that they would. She had already spoken to them and told them I was dying.

They took me in right away. It was confirmed that I had acute liver failure and might not survive. I prayed again, "God, please heal me or take me now." I didn't die, so he wanted me to live, for some reason. Sheila stayed until she couldn't stay anymore. She had to get back to her life. Some days, after undergoing many tests and procedures, I was told I would not survive without a liver transplant. They showed me a picture of my liver. It looked like a big clump of black cottage cheese. There was one tiny spot that was still pink. Doctors said it was not enough to regenerate my liver.

I refused to consider a transplant. I did not want to take a good liver away from someone who deserved it. I didn't...I had done this to myself! This time when I prayed, I was praying with faith, hope, and belief that God could save me or take me. No other choices existed for me. I was at the end of my earthly life! God's plan was different. He saved me to fulfill a purpose of some kind.

My hospital adventures kept coming. Several months passed that I barely remember. Then one day, I woke up, tried to get out of the hospital bed, and fell on my butt. I could not stand or walk. IVs had been pulled out all over the place, blood was everywhere. All I could think was, Why can't I walk?

I was released to a nearby nursing home. The doctor who was treating me at the time knew I had no place to go, and the hospital wasn't going to keep me there for free anymore. He was one of my miracles. God put him into my life to help heal me. I know this and am forever grateful to him. I don't remember his name, just his dedication to me. Pro bono!

After six months in the nursing home, undergoing physical therapy to learn how to walk again, I was wheelchair bound. Everywhere I went, I had to roll! I kept praying earnestly all this time, and eventually, I could get around with a walker. After a few weeks of that, I left my walker in my room and walked to therapy on my own two feet. I almost fell several times, and it seemed to take me forever to get down that hallway, but I was walking. And I kept practicing and practicing. I kept thanking God for my progress. He was the guiding force behind all of the care I received. I know this in my soul! Know why? Because I had no one and nothing else to help me. Period.

Somewhere along the way, I started to realize I could recover. I needed to feed my soul and starve my cravings for alcohol. I asked God to remove the desire to drink from me, and with persistent prayer and doing the footwork laid out by him, I began to have some moments of clarity in my thinking. I was able to make the decision to admit my mistakes, own my behavior, and be willing to believe that I was not in control. I thought I was, but no. God has a plan for me. My life will go according to his plan, no matter how I try to mess it up. I do the footwork and keep on doing the next right thing, and I will see what the plan is eventually. In the meantime, I have to stay sober, practice what I preach, and believe my prayers will be answered in God's time.

I had made attempts throughout my drinking career to get sober and stay sober. I went to a couple of thirty-day treatments for alcoholism. I stayed the whole time, each time, counting the days until I could get the hell out of there. Each time, as the period came to a close on these programs of recovery, professionals urged me to seek longer and more thorough programs. They said I had to keep working on the character defects that I supposedly had that made me drink in the first place.

Mental illness is a big part of the disease of alcoholism. I refused each time to stay even one day longer. I thought I had learned enough about this disease to stay sober. Wrong! Not until I finally got into a residential rehab that was based on doing the twelve steps of Alcoholics Anonymous did I truly understand the scope of my problem. In addition to the Ten Commandments, the twelve steps were written by a man with God guiding his way.

In addition to regular AA meetings I had to attend, the programs focused on spiritual fitness as well. The spiritual work was of key importance to success in my recovery. One day in rehab, we were standing in a big circle, reciting the Lord's Prayer, as we did at the end of every meeting at the rehab home. On one of these occasions, I started shaking, trembling, and getting cold chills all up and down my body. There was no doubt in my mind that it was God. He was telling me he had my back. I could be vulnerable and I could be humble and I could heal my soul if I prayed and asked for his help. After that experience, I started crying uncontrollably.

I cried for several days in a row until I had no more tears left to cry. I was finally ready to let go of my hurtful feelings and my fears. I trusted in God's will for me and let him take over my worrying for me. I prayed for salvation minute by minute and begged for his strength and power to make me well.

I am beginning to understand that my life was already planned. God has it all in his control. My little life is important in the scheme of things. I truly believe that I am here on this earth today because of the grace of God and his plans for me. I can't wait to realize what he has in mind. In the meantime, I want to live each day to the fullest. To me, that means doing for others, doing for myself, and being happy on the inside and out. Being angry, sad, *tired, and grumpy is a waste of my time.*

I don't know how much longer God will keep me here, but I know he wants me to be happy. He loves me, no matter what. He made me imperfect so I could improve and build a relationship with him. I believe this so strongly. I refuse to deny myself the joys of being reasonable, fair, caring, and just plain old having as much fun as I can while I'm still able to. I have certainly done many things in my life that not many people get to do. I am favored, in a way, by the spirit of God.

I'm celebrating over ten years of sobriety. The first couple of years were the toughest. The urge to drink lingered in the back of my mind. I kept praying for the urge to go away, and it did, eventually—in God's time, not mine. I had a peace and a serene feeling that I had never had before. God works in mysterious ways and leads us through some briar patches along our trek to being the best person we can be—the person God wants us to be.

We are all here for a purpose, and everything happens for a reason in God's world. He let me see the way to get my life back. He healed my soul and my liver so I could be here today, writing all of this stuff. I am grateful for each day I wake up sober, and I do my best to stay in the moment of the day I am in at the time.

I expected a miracle. I got more than my fair share...my liver healed and functions normally today, I don't have any desire or urge to drink. I am with my husband of forty-nine years, and we are best friends and lovers. We can live on our retirement and social security funds, we live in a wonderful house on a wonderful street in a wonderful little town in Tennessee. It's the exact opposite of the situation I had been in. If you don't believe in miracles, you should.

Love the Addict; Hate the Addiction

Chapter 4

I Can-Cer Vive

The room was quiet. There was a chill in the air, and mom and I just sat there quietly, dumbfounded. There is only one single word I can use to describe my emotion: *Panic.* I felt it set in as my mom and I held hands and held our breath. Just a few short minutes before, I had been told that I needed a mammogram because tests had shown something on my breast exam. I had shown up for my yearly exam like always, and the lady came in to the room and did her normal routine. After that, she said, "I will be right back. We need to keep you a little longer." And that was it. No explanation, nothing. She left me in this cold room with a million thoughts running marathons over and over in my mind. I felt so confused.

Two seconds later, the doctor came in and said, "We need to do another test. Go across the hall, and they will do your mammogram." Mammogram? I felt numb. I had heard the word mammogram before and I knew it meant something serious. I was twenty-eight and had never even thought about having a mammogram at that age. I had heard that they were painful and also that they were associated with breast cancer. But that's all I knew. I felt like all I wanted to do was run away from that hospital as fast as I could, but of course, I couldn't. And, as I usually did when fear came over me, I just froze.

So many thoughts ran through my mind as minutes that went by seemed like hours. I was in so much shock that I couldn't even cry. We had just found out a few days before that my mom had been diagnosed with skin cancer and she would be going in to have it removed. My dad and I had gone as her support, and they told her about the different options that they could use to remove the cancer.

As we sat there waiting in the silence I reflected back on what had just happened with mom. Music has always been my outlet for pain, so I remember how I had just been at home crying and singing Martina McBride's song "I'm Gonna Love You Through It" over and over again while I banged it out on the piano keys, tears streaming down my face. At the same time begging God to just make my mom be okay. My mom is my very best friend, and I was so afraid. I didn't do this around her because I didn't want to scare her, but my heart was terrified. I couldn't imagine living my life without my mother, my rock, my best friend. When they first diagnosed her they didn't tell us much. In fact, because it was a Friday afternoon we had to wait through the weekend before we got any details at all. We didn't know what type of cancer it was or anything—whether it was going to stay put or whether it had spread or was capable of spreading.

When she first told me what the doctor had said, I felt numb. It didn't even feel real. I heard the word, **CANCER** but it didn't make sense. I watched as my dad too was afraid, although he would never say it out loud. I could see it in his eyes. My parents are best friends. They have been married for thirty-six years, and they have everything that I hope one day to have in my relationship with the man who I marry. They still date, laugh, hold hands, and inspire each other. He couldn't live his life without her, and I knew that his heart was terrified as well.

As mom and I sat there in the cold and lifeless doctor's office, reflecting on our situations and waiting to be taken in to get my mammogram, holding my hand, and in a very matter of fact tone she said, "No matter what this is, we are both going to get through this together. If it's cancer, we will fight it together. We are strong and we can get through anything." I felt a wave of relief wash over me. I felt strength come over my spirit, and I knew she was right. I was not going to let this get me down. We would fight this head on. She would fight her battle, and I would fight mine if I needed to, and together, we would be victorious. No matter what! We had to live for each other. We couldn't give up now.

I still remember the experience like yesterday. The nurse must have called my name quite a few times because once I got to where she was I could hear the impatience in her tone. But then she looked at my fearful eyes and down at her chart. Her eyes filled with concern. She said softly, "Take off your clothes' top half and put on this gown. And leave the front part open." I remember being alone in this empty room, seeing this big machine in front of me, and thinking, How could this happen? Why am I here? What if it's cancer? Will I be okay? Then I thought, Well, I eat well. I do exercise sometimes; I always do my checkups. I know I take care of myself. But I'm too young for this. They usually don't give your first mammogram til your forties, and here I am, twenty-eight, and I have so much life ahead of me. Why, God, why?

Then I slowly went into a prayer begging God to let everything be okay and not let me have breast cancer. I slowly felt the fear creep in as the nurse placed my breast on the machine. It was cold and I felt a chill run through me, unsure if it was from the machine or from what I knew the results could be. Either way I cringed, and felt the tears well up in my eyes. I expressed my fear, and she said, "Not to worry. It will be over soon enough." This machine grabbed my breast and squeezed as if trying to squeeze the life right out of me. Then I had to reach up and grab the bar on top of the machine as they angled it so they could get a different profile. I held on to the side until my knuckles hurt. I just wanted this horrible nightmare to be over. I couldn't get my clothes on fast enough so I could get back to my mom's loving embrace. I don't care how old you are there's no safer feeling than being in your mother's arms.

When I got out of the room, I cried for a long time. Once I had gotten my strength back and had stopped bawling, we got up and headed to the car. It would be some time before they would let me know anything, and I was terrified. After I cried those tears, I chose at that moment that I wasn't going to let it get me down anymore. Worrying would just make it worse, and it wasn't going to change anything. I was going to be strong, and I realized whatever the outcome was, I had two amazing people who loved me and supported me, and no matter what we were going to get through whatever challenge I might face. I am happy to say a week later we got word that everything was okay. I was breast-cancer free. I had never felt so much relief in my life.

So, in our household, there was one down and one to go. But Mom and I stuck to our promise that we were going to get through it all and be victorious, and we did. We both found the strength and our warrior within.

I want to take a moment before we get to the next section to talk about all people who fight cancer. They are heroes, plain and simple. I had the pleasure of hearing the stories of some cancer survivors recently, and they are incredible. What amazes me is how much strength and fearlessness that every one of them possesses. Even though my mom didn't have a terminal type, it still affected her. Cancer is scary, and it doesn't matter what type you have. And it's so prevalent in our society. We will all, at some point, know someone or be someone who is affected by this awful invader. But people have to realize that they are never fighting alone. This disease is not a one-person battle. We are all fighting it in some way, and we need to help fund research to find cures and help those we love, any way we can. According to the American Cancer Society and cancer.org, in 2019, there will be 1,762,450 new cancer cases diagnosed and 606,880 cancer deaths in the United States.

https://www.cancer.org/

"Cancer does not have a face until it's yours or someone you know"

-Anthony Del Monte

Life story by Linda Martinez, My Mom

A number of years ago, I discovered a small red bump on my left cheek, just below the corner of my eye. I expected the blemish to go away quickly, but after many months, it persisted. It eventually started to get larger, scaly, and very annoying, so I went to a dermatologist to see what to do about it.

To my surprise, the dermatologist told me she wanted to do a biopsy and did so right there, on the spot.

So my concern went from, "What do I do about a pimple gone wild? To, could this be cancer?" It was a very long week of wondering. When the results finally came back, the biopsy confirmed the worst: it was cancer.

Thus, my journey began with skin cancer. My first step was a lot of praying and knowing that I was right with God, no matter what happened.

The biopsy revealed that I had squamous-cell carcinoma. Up to this point in my life, I thought all skin cancers were the same. I didn't realize that there are also basal-cell carcinoma and melanoma. All three are very different, with different beginnings and different endings.

So, my husband said, "Let's call Uncle John"—who is a doctor of pathology—"and find out what he can tell us about squamous-cell carcinoma and how to get treatment for it." Uncle John explained that basal-cell carcinoma is the most common form of skin cancer and the least invasive. Squamous-cell carcinoma can be more invasive and not only affects the skin, but also surrounding tissues and bones, and it can also spread to lymph nodes. So his recommendation was to get the cancerous tissue removed.

I began thinking back to my childhood. Could that bright-red sunburn that covered my face and my back and turned into huge blisters and that caused me to be nauseous and run a fever with chills, have had anything to do with my condition now?

I was not ready to say good-bye to my dear husband and daughter, so I began my search for the best way to remove the cancer. My first appointment was with a plastic surgeon. Since the surgery was going to affect a large portion of my left cheek, I wanted to get the best possible results. I was concerned that I would look hideous with a large scar on my cheek and scare away potential clients and their children (I sell real estate). But the plastic surgeon could not guarantee that he could remove all the cancer with his surgery.

I was not giving up on my search for a way to remove the cancer permanently. On the Internet, I discovered a procedure called MOHS surgery, which allows a doctor to carefully remove tissue layer by layer until cancer-free tissue is reached. Next, I looked for the best MOHS surgeon in my area. He not only removed the cancer but also did such a wonderful job that today; it is hard to tell that I had surgery at all.

I feel so blessed that I made it through this journey to share my story.

But here is the rest of the story. I discovered that one in five Americans develop skin cancer by the age of 70. More people are diagnosed with skin cancer each year in the U.S. than all other cancers combined. More than 9,500 people in the U.S. are diagnosed with skin cancer every day. More than 2 people of the disease die every hour. More than 4 million cases of basal-cell carcinoma are diagnosed in the U.S. each year, along with more than 1 million cases of squamous-cell carcinoma. An estimated 192,310 cases of melanoma will be diagnosed in the U.S. in 2019. Most melanomas and other skin cancers can be attributed to exposure to ultraviolet radiation from the sun. On average, a person's risk for melanoma doubles if he or she has had more than five sunburns, but just one blistering sunburn in childhood or adolescence more than doubles a person's chances of developing melanoma later in life. (Facts published by the Skin Cancer Foundation.)

https://www.skincancer.org/

If there is a possibility that you have a skin condition that is not normal for you, please go have it checked. It's all about getting early diagnosis and treatment.

Life story by John Martinez, My Dad

When you are healthy and your family is healthy and you hear that someone you know has been diagnosed with cancer, if you are like me, you hear it and you feel it a bit and somehow wish it were not true. Then you move on with your day.

Then one day, you get a call from someone really close to you—my wife in this case—and you hear her saying, "I have been diagnosed with cancer." At first, I felt the same way as I might have for that someone else I knew, but in a moment, I heard it again in my head and then in my gut, my heart, and my soul. What? What did she just say? Oh my God, what does this mean? What did they say? Where is the cancer? What should we do? How serious is it? All these questions ran through my mind.

I rarely feel fear or dread, but her voice saying "I have cancer" set my system into high gear. Fear and dread were there in an instant. I am a positive, "glass is half full" kind of guy, but I could hear in her voice that she was scared. I wanted to not let my fear and dread show. I felt that my positive attitude would help me reassure her that things would be okay and that I was there for her, that I loved her, and that I would help her every step of the way.

She had cancer on her face, and removing it would require surgery. She was worried about how horrible it would be to face the world if the surgery caused major scarring. She was depressed about all of this, and I was worried about the effect the scarring might have on her soul. She was worried about whether they would be able to get it all. The effects of not getting it all were quite serious. We needed a great outcome.

My wife is very thorough with research, and she found the best cancer doctors in our area. She also researched various techniques that could rid her of the cancer, and we discussed the pros and cons of each. She was able to find some comfort from other church members who had gone through similar surgeries. We found the doctor, she settled on the technique, and we scheduled the surgery.

The surgery involved removing and examining a layer of skin in the diagnosed area, continuing with one layer at time until it removed a layer without cancer. Then the reconstruction of the facial region would begin. I was glad when they reported that there were not many layers that needed to be removed and that she would be cancer free.

My wait for her to recover enough for us to take her home felt like a long time. You never know what can happen, what they will find, or what you might have to face as you go through something like this, waiting for the results. They did remove all of the cancer. The reconstruction was done masterfully, and in the end there was no scarring—of the face or soul.

I was glad to have her back happy, healthy, and cancer free. Sometimes, it is you who needs to be strong and make sure that those around you never give up as they fight their way through life's traumas.

In some ways, it was my cancer too.

I Can-Cer Vive

Chapter 5

Wounds to Wisdom

My Voice

By: Angela Martinez

Words come flying at me from every direction
I held my tongue as a way to keep my own protection
I pushed my feelings back and felt the tension
I wish there was just one time
But there's too many times to mention

I became a prisoner lost in translation
I lost myself in the abuse
And forgot about elation
I somehow felt that's what I deserved at the time
But knowing that I didn't
The punishment never fit the crime

I would tolerate things that I never thought I could
I went through things that I never thought I would
I endured pain that I never knew existed
And at the same time I never even resisted

I stay quiet just to observe and reflect what I've been through
If given the chance I would do a re-do
But that's not possible so I do what I can do
And that's to give a voice to that girl that I once knew

My voice will be heard it's no longer just inside
I will say what I think and feel and deliver it with pride
No one else is going to ever be allowed to decide
What happens to my body, to my heart, or to my mind

"Turn your wounds into wisdom"

-Oprah

Life story by Joanna Vasquez

2:04 a.m., Wednesday, October 28, 2015. I wake up next to my husband, thinking, Gosh, it's about the fourth time I have to go to the bathroom. Will I ever sleep again? Should I wake him up this time to help me roll out of bed, or should I struggle through it like I have the last nine months? My feet are so swollen, I can't turn anymore. When will this end? Hopefully today, because I am finally being induced.

6:30 a.m. The nurse tells me, "Mrs. Vasquez, I have your medication to start your induction. We are starting early because your test results show that the fluid you have is actually amniotic fluid. Here is your first dose of misoprostol. In a short period, your contractions will become more frequent and stronger."

3:00 p.m. "Our goal is to get you to deliver before the twenty-four-hour mark, Mrs. Vasquez. It reduces the chance of infection since your water already ruptured."

7:00 p.m., Thursday, October 29. There is a change of shift for the nurses. The same nurse from the night before asks, "Why haven't you delivered?"

7:30 p.m. "Mrs. Vasquez, you have met the criteria for severe preeclampsia. Your kidneys are shutting down, you are not producing urine, we have carefully monitored your blood pressure, and we have to treat you at this point. We will start with magnesium."

8:15 p.m. "Your baby is showing indications of fetal distress, and we must deliver this baby within the next fifteen minutes or we will have to do an emergency cesarean section."

9:40 p.m. It's my first trip to the operating room. I was there before as a nursing student but never as a patient. It is a sterile place; the nurses and doctors work fast, and they are disconnected. It's cold and unfamiliar when you are the patient, and I am scared, but I am not sure why. Seems silly, because people do this every day. I am at a great hospital. What could go wrong? Valentina will finally be here. Calm down, Joanna. It is finally that moment. I can finally be done being pregnant and have that sweet baby in my arms. You are a nurse, and you take care of others, but this time people can take care of you, and you will have a sweet baby to hold. Don't be scared. Your kidneys will go back to normal, and your blood pressures will stabilize and hopefully, this swelling will too. Just breathe.

9:48 p.m. Valentina is born. She's quiet, observant. My husband Adrian is crying. She has normal Apgar scores. Life seems surreal!

10:30 a.m., Friday, October 30. Knock, knock—Adrian walks in the door. He looks rested, but I realize right away that he has missed his promotion ceremony at work! This week, he became a captain for LAFD! He meets baby Valentina once again, who is wearing her "My daddy is Captain Vasquez" onesie. Dad is in disbelief. Sigh. Life is perfect!

10:30 p.m., Saturday, October 31. "I can't stand the pain! Please call the doctor! I feel like something is wrong." People have cesarean sections every day. Why can't I urinate?

The nurse responds, "The doctor will be paged; however, whatever you are experiencing is normal. C-sections can be painful; It just takes time. We can medicate you for now and tell the rounding doctors in the morning."

12:00 p.m., Monday, November 1. "Mrs. Vasquez, thank you for choosing us to be your birth place. We hope you had a great experience. All of your current symptoms are normal. Call us if you need to."

They say that having a baby is like running a marathon. Well, at least that's what I heard before getting pregnant. But I never understood what it meant until I actually did it. On President's Day, I delivered the most exciting news to my husband! He was going to be a dad, and our beach-living life was only going to get more exciting. When you are young and you have your career all figured out, a fun social life...what could possibly go wrong? Life seemed absolutely perfect.

On October 29, 2015, we had our baby! She was amazing—so new, so fragile, and so perfect! I could not wait to get to know her more, be home with her, plan the holidays with her, and enjoy time off with my husband at home, just the three of us, at the most precious time in our lives. I made it home on Monday, November 1 from the hospital to start my new life as a mommy.

On November 5, 2015, my entire existence changed. I felt sensations in my every nerve, and a kind of fear I had not known existed. I woke up that morning knowing in my heart that something was wrong. I looked in the mirror as I washed my face, and I saw something I had never seen in myself before. I went to Valentina's bassinet that morning, and I was afraid to pick her up. How could I do that and possibly say good-bye? How could I let her go and put her back down? I had just met her. Was I leaving so soon?

But I finally picked her up. I held her tight and whispered in her ear, "I promise to come back. It may not be today, but I will be back."

I felt numb as I forced myself down the stairs leading to the front door. It was an internal disconnect from my heart. I had to think and act, not feel. I had to force myself to get in the car and go into the ER, not knowing what to expect that morning.

Friends had started to show up to my hospital room to extend their support, even though they didn't know why. A surgeon arrived and asked to talk privately to my husband and me. Evening came. I had been hoping I was wrong, but my worst fears were coming true. A surgeon came into my room and asked to privately talk to my husband and me. He put his head down and explained that my symptoms all indicated that I had a deadly, rapidly growing infection called necrotizing fasciitis. I had never heard of it. I just know it sounded bad, and I didn't doubt it, based on my quick vital changes, the rapid increase in my heartbeat, and the blackish blister spreading on my lower abdomen. It looked like I was rotting internally like a piece of fruit.

The surgeon wanted to operate on me right away because it was life threatening and I could die. He had another mom with an ectopic pregnancy waiting in the ER, but my case was first. As a nurse, I knew what that meant. The mom downstairs could have bad internal bleeding at any moment, but my condition was even more critical—I could die sooner. I felt like I was drowning in the ocean all by myself with no one around to save me. It was like the moment when you are about to rear-end another car and you slam on the brakes, praying you will stop and you can breathe again. It was a real nightmare. Please, God, this can't be happening! Wake up, Joanna!

After I heard the surgeon, I went numb again. The doom felt like a pile of bricks on my chest. I couldn't breathe; the numbness in my limbs almost hurt. I felt the emotional pain in my joints, sank into the bed, and felt like I was just falling and falling. You know it's not a dream anymore when you can hear your husband burst into tears. But I did not. I stayed calm.

There was a ticking clock on the wall. I had never paid attention to clocks like I did that day. A part of me wanted to pass out, because I could not bear what I was living through. But the sound of the clock as the second hand moved made me realize how precious each second of life can be.

I did not want to say this out loud, so I told myself, "I can't die. I am a brand-new mother. I have a baby at home, and we are still getting to know each other. She needs me. She needs me because her dad won't know what to do with her alone. Neither will her grandparents. Where will she live? Who will feed her and dress her and teach her the things I want her to know? Who will take her to school? Who will teach her to walk? Who will she talk to when she is alone? Who will help her buy her wedding dress? I have to see her graduate and her first recital, be there when she comes home from school upset. I can't do this to her! I can't die." And then came the despair. It had only been a few minutes, but it seemed eternal.

My nurse that night and I had just met when I came from the ER. She was nice, sweet, and pregnant. She looked stressed and scared for me. All the nurses did. They were not your usual nurses, disconnected and ready to go home at the end of their shift. They were kind, they were hurting, they were scared. They were crying. My initial thought was, Nurses don't cry unless they have to.

I was wheeled to the OR. I met my surgeon right at the red lines on the floor for the first time. Only those who are in special attire can walk past these lines. It all feels like a blur now, but I remember scribbling my consent for the surgery, barely knowing what I was doing. Was I signing my life away because I would not wake up from this? Or was I trusting those whom I had just met, telling me they would do their best to try to save me? And from there, my husband and I parted ways. I promised to see him soon. I closed my eyes and don't remember a thing after that. I imagine that it was cold, lonely, painful, and hectic, like my first time in the operating room. I felt alone, shattered, and completely vulnerable.

A few days later, I opened my eyes. I was lying flat and gagging because I had something in my throat. I couldn't see anything except a small tunnel of light. I felt panic, but I couldn't move. My hands had been restrained, and my body felt disconnected because I couldn't get up like I had for the past thirty-one years. Where am I? I heard beeping and people talking in the hallway.

At some point, someone must have knocked me out again, because whatever had been in my throat was now out. Life felt like a circle of confusion. I didn't recognize any faces and still didn't know where I was. I was breathing, though. And then I saw that clock again up on the wall. The second hand was still moving. I was alive or in a dream...or heaven had clocks!

The person at my bedside...I wish I could remember his or her name or face. I tried to communicate, but I realized again that my body wasn't working. I could barely talk or move. That person placed a phone to my ear, and a man said, "Hello." It was my husband. That was when I knew I was still on earth and in the hospital. I had kept my promise to him that I would not leave. I was still here, still alive.

I must have fallen in and out of consciousness, because I felt like I had blackouts. The next time I opened my eyes, I had friends at my bedside. The most random of people whom I rarely saw were standing by me, telling me it was going to be okay. I think I talked to them, I'm not sure. I just know they had pale, blank looks on their faces and ran out of words. Finally, my husband walked in. There was that guy, a familiar face, sobbing again.

The rest of that day is a cloud of memories. I just remember it being so painful. I couldn't move. I could barely talk. My throat and every inch of my body were in pain. Two nurses had to help turn me, and when I patted down my abdomen to try to figure out what my surgery incision felt like, my dry hands felt plastic. My abdomen was still open but covered with something. I could feel my organs, not my skin. Not my baby kicking.

Someone then broke the news. I had had a surgical debridement, which meant they had cut out all of the infected tissue, including skin and belly button, and had removed my uterus. I was so overwhelmed and weak, but it was the least of my worries at the moment.

More and more family and friends came and went. My uncle, whom I had not spoken with in years, walked in. He was nice to me and consoled me. My parents were there, my sister, my friends. Just no baby—the only person I was interested in seeing.

The day became clearer, and I could comprehend more. I had had two surgeries and needed one more on Tuesday. The plastic on my abdomen was protecting it and helping it heal, but on Tuesday I would be given a skin graft to close it. Honestly, I questioned my ability to keep myself alive that day.

I began to heal every day from there, making physical progress. My infection was slowly subsiding, but the emotional pain and fear seemed to be getting worse. Three and a half weeks—

that's how long I was away from home. Every day was different, every hour changed, every single second felt like it was the worst time in my life.

I questioned God's plan. I cried in despair. I felt like I couldn't breathe. Sometimes, I admit, I wanted to die of the pain. But when I closed my eyes, I pictured her—that face I had said good-bye to, that small girl who needed her mom and my promise to come home.

I remember sitting on my hospital bed a few days before discharge. It was sunny outside, and I could see the clear skies. The room was quiet—so quiet, the anxiety began to escalate. Patients usually like quiet so they can rest. This hospital was so darn good at providing quiet for patients that it bothered me. I wanted to quit. I could no longer take the agony and became so mad.

It was four days before Christmas, the happiest time of year. How could it be the worst time in my life? How did having a baby correlate with such feelings? Why me? For a long time, those were my questions. They were the reason I cried everywhere I went and why I could not be left alone for long periods, the reason I jumped out of my sleep, felt like something bad was about to happen, and the reason I questioned God's plan.

It took me a long time to come to terms with it and not replay it in my brain over and over again. To overcome a situation like this, you must find a way to stop bargaining. If this experience had never happened, would I be where I am today?

Today, I feel like I can do anything! I am stronger than I used to be. I am wiser, I am complete. If I had to do it again, I would, because there is nothing a mother will not do for her children. I have learned that there are few problems in life that have no solution. Instead of focusing on why God did this to me, I have learned to accept it as what God did for me. He saved me. He healed me, he encouraged me, and he didn't leave me. He allowed me to stay here on this earth and overcome my weaknesses, my pain, this nightmare. Valentina is a year old now! We survived, and together, we are thankful, hopeful, and so blessed.

Chapter 6

Love

Love is what life is all about. We were all made in the image of love. You can love your spouse, family, friends, but most important you need to love yourself. I love the Bible's explanation of what love is: "Love is patient, Love is kind...it always protects, always trusts, always hopes, always perseveres. Love never fails" (1 Cor. 13:4).

I think the Bible's definition of love is the purest but the hardest thing to live up to. We all use the word "love" so often and try to define in it in our own way, but I think a lot of us fail to understand what it really means. Some use it to express romantic and passionate feelings toward someone. Some people use it to mean affection in a platonic relationship. Some people use the word to create deception to get people to do what they want. Some people use it to define their feelings toward themselves and remove self-judgment, focusing on the things that matter most. Some show it by the care, concern, and passion they have for their children. Some show it not for a person but for a goal or accomplishment they desire. Love is everywhere and in everything.

We all want love. Many songs, movies, and stories originate from the idea of love. Love is not just a feeling; it's an action. It's something that you do. The feeling is a wonderful, never-ending feeling of pure happiness. I must admit, I am a hopeless romantic, and I love the idea of love. I fell in love with the song "I Will Always Love You" when I heard Whitney belt out the first words acapella "If

I, should stay" it struck my young heart in a way that I had never been hit before. I listened to it over and over. It was a love song but yet filled with so much pain. That song taught me that love isn't always easy. It's funny because as a child I never knew that it was a country song written by the amazing Dolly Parton. But as I grew up and learned that about the song, and that somehow made even more sense to me why my heart fell in love with it. Country music has always been a part of me even when I didn't know it.

We all love differently and express that through something called our love language. According to Gary Chapman who wrote the book "The Five Love Languages," there are 5 ways to express love. We can express it by showing love through words, physical and emotional intimacy, spending time with someone, giving gifts, or doing acts of kindness. If both love languages are not being considered by both people that it can truly affect relationships in major ways.

My biggest love language is words of affirmation because I am so in tune with songwriting and music. It's all focused around lyrics, and that's the best way that I can express myself and my emotions. If you want to get into my heart, use words. But the most important thing I have learned is that there have to be actions behind the words. Otherwise, they have no meaning. I challenge you to go to the 5 love languages website and find out what your love language is. You will live a more fulfilling life and have a better relationship when you do.

https://www.5lovelanguages.com/

Through my experiences of being that hopeless romantic and having my heart broken I have learned to look at love differently than before. I still believe in romance but I believe that love is a choice; and it is the biggest choice you will ever make. When you think of love as a choice and not just a fateful event, you bring analysis into the picture. Analysis is important because then you can make an educated decision with your heart and mind on whether this person is someone you can love forever and not base it on rainbows and butterflies.

Everyone has flaws. You just have to decide which ones you are willing to deal with and make compromises on. Can you see yourself growing old with this person? Are they good with money? What's the relationship with their family like? When things aren't in that honeymoon phase anymore and life's problems arise does this person show you they know how to negotiate and compromise and work through the hard times. When you are sick will they stand by your side and take care of you and help you heal? Does this person display integrity, honesty, and have respect for them and you? You fall in lust because of chemistry and hormones and feel attraction when you like how a person looks physically, but when love really grows is when you discover the core values of who a person really is and determine together whether you are both a good match for one another based on your values, wants, and needs in life.

Love is not just a one-time decision. When you do finally choose to fall in love with someone and give them your heart, you must make the choice to wake up and love that person every single day. You have to let them know they are the one you chose and that you will always abide by that decision every single second of every day for the rest of your life.

For the first time in my life I found that kind of love. One that I know is unconditional and worth waking up for everyday. Making the decision to love this person more than I did the day before is easy. That person understands me without me even trying to explain things. They know what my heart feels without me having to say a word. Their values match mine, and the vision of the future is brighter than it has ever been. I am so thankful that God has finally shown me who that person is. ME! It took me a long time to find her but now I see her every day when I look in the mirror and I know I am stronger and more ready for life than I have ever been. Now I am ready to take on the role of being a mother to my little miracle and be the warrior that I have always had inside me.

"Love Always Finds A Way"

-Guy Finley

Life story by Ana Maria Castaneda

I did not see it coming. It hit me before I even knew how to put words to it. There was no warning, no greeting. And right as I discovered that it was love, it morphed into the most intense heartbreak I had ever experienced. It was the summer of 2015, and I had fallen in love, a fierce love, all to have it taken away from me as quickly as it was given. But the most surprising thing of it all was that God was placing me on a path to a love I only ever thought existed in dreams.

This was not the first heartbreak I had experienced. Everyone I had known over the span of the twenty-five years I had lived, was teaching me the absolute meaning of who God is. God is love. He kept appearing to me through the heartbreaks, someone who consoled my soul and kept me hopeful for a lesson learned and a higher purpose. A little bit about myself, I am a Latina woman who grew up with Latin family values. I come from a large immigrant family. I and my eight siblings are first-generation American citizens and were first-generation college students. We each felt the responsibility of growing a legacy for our family here in the States as we saw our parents make the best of their situation as immigrants.

My first heartbreak was when I was nine years old. My mother told me that the father I was growing up with was not my biological father but my stepfather. Talk about ripping a heart to shreds at the ripe age of nine. That's when I pieced together why the only family we had living nearby treated me like an outsider all my life. They knew I was not their blood. Yet my dad never let his family's behavior take away from the love he had for me. My favorite thing to this day is when he mentions that I am his eldest to anyone who he introduces me to. We like to smile at each other when people mention the "family resemblance". My parents worked hard at making me feel like I was no different from my other siblings. My mother's and father's love taught me a lot about the love a parent has for a child regardless of outside circumstances. It all made sense, the love of a parent and child—a fundamental love that helped shape the person I would become. After all, God is our Father, and through every stage of life, he holds that same relationship with us, that of a father and us, His children. My parents' love had helped me understand God and His love for me and my existence.

The next heartbreak was the inevitable first breakup. We were babies in high school when our love began, but we became a bit distant my junior year, when he was a freshman in college. A whole new pond with a whole new species of fish apparently led him to cheat on me and shatter my heart into pieces. At this point, we had been dating for two years. We tried recovering from the transgressions for the following three years, but it didn't work out. That rollercoaster of dysfunction led me to learn a thing or two about love, trust, and friendship.

The hurt and confusion that God had placed in my heart allowed me to be open and create strong friendships with people I met in college. There's something so good that comes from having a close-knit group of girlfriends. We did so much together and loved each other unconditionally. Yes, there were some moments of conflict, but over the course of the next seven years, we laughed together through fun times and cried together through tough times. I had read numerous articles about how friendships become life long after the seven-year mark. A lot of us even took note of the moment when Facebook told us we had been friends online for seven years, because we had been friends in person that long. It was exciting, because it meant we all were most likely stuck with each other for the rest of our lives. We love each other! It all made sense. The love I had learned to cherish through friendships was the love of sisters through Christ and in Christ. This was God's gift of family who did not have to be connected by blood but by heart.

For a span of time, my heart was healed from the past and

was now focused on the future. I was enjoying my friendships and focused on finishing college so I could start a career, something outside of the plans that most women from either side of my family had chosen for themselves. You see, I come from a long line of Latina homemakers and housewives...professional stay-at-home mothers, if you will.

My Latina culture is known for the outstanding mothers that have come before us. I had looked forward to making a family and providing a feminine touch at home. Being a matriarch of a family comes with its pros and cons, and from my families' standpoint, matriarchy does not come with a career. Your career is your family. But I aspired to be a business owner and a mother—to incorporate the deep family traditions I was taught from my Latin culture and the modern concept of being independent and providing for myself through a career that I learned from school and American society. I was on a good route to accomplishing my dreams, enrolled in a university and working part time at jobs that would help me to make the best of the career I was going for. But I did not realize I was on the path to a new heartbreak that had everything to do with my goals. It brought them to a screeching halt so that I could tend to the damage this particular heartbreak caused: that of my parents' divorce.

The casualties of this divorce were my brothers and sisters, my studies, my future career, and the relationship I had started with someone whom I thought embodied the family values I wanted in a husband. I went through a few years of heartbreak as I witnessed my mother try to recover from the divorce. My family was left in shambles, and my focus had completely shifted to me and my family's needs.

My studies became a lower priority, and I found that I didn't have the support I needed in my relationship. At a glacial pace, I ended up getting out of it. It had turned hostile and toxic, but I had been blind to it for a while. My heart had seemed to have found a safe haven while I endured the pain from my family breaking apart, so it was easy to let some things slide in the relationship. Its end did cause a deeper pain in me, but I knew I had to move forward and help with easing the pain my family was going through.

Some time passed, and I found myself healing for the better.

Maybe I've left out a lot of detail about each heartbreak, but I mention them only to preface the knowledge about God's grace and love that I learned along the way to prepare me for the biggest heartbreak I had to face. In the summer of 2015, I fell in love with a friend I never expected to fall in love with. He is tall, handsome, and a lover of nature and all things good. I cherished his mind because he did not concern himself with the shallow, surface-level idiocies our generation seems to immerse itself in.

My plan for that fall was to move to California in search of a new life after all the heartbreaks I had gone through. It was time to make my dreams come true, be a business owner, and grow my livelihood in the Latino community. I felt I could do that in California, where I would be close to some great work contacts and the ocean—which has always tugged at my soul. As I was still in Tennessee, preparing for my move, I spent the summer bidding my good-bye to the state's rolling hills, hiking and swimming. My friend joined me in my adventures to hike beautiful spots and swim in fun places, but we were only friends. Since I was moving away for the next two to five years to pursue a different life, we felt there was no reason to start a committed relationship.

It all happened so suddenly. I fell straight into the love I had wanted to reserve for my next relationship. God had allowed our friendship to blossom, yet I did not know what to do with it when I left. I still planned to move, but I could not leave without saying the words that I loved him. I did not expect him to tell me he loved me too. I only wanted him to know how much I loved him and how thankful I was for his companionship. After the pain my heart had felt from my parents' divorce and my own failed relationships, I had learned to speak my mind if my heart were to be heard.

The month leading up to my move was not turning out the way I had envisioned. My friend stopped returning my calls or texting me to see how I was, and I was left confused. I had mustered up the courage to say the words "I love you," but my opportunity had been taken away. Why the sudden shift? Why go from constant connection to absolute darkness? I knew something was not right. It was not like him to leave me in the dark. Two weeks of no communication went by, and that was when I found out I was pregnant. God loves to surprise us in the moments when we least expect it. I had always looked forward to motherhood, but not like this. I could not even tell the father of my unborn child that we were expecting a little soul to join us on this earth. Heartbreak. Utmost heartbreak.

I reached out to his family. If I could not reach him, I knew who could. What I came to find out through these efforts of communication was only going to wrench my heart to the point of no return. His family let me know that it was a very dark time in his life and that his health was being affected. I felt I was dying, dying to myself, dying to this world. How had I not realized his health had been declining? I looked back at little moments from our summer, and I saw symptoms that I had not been aware of before.

It all made sense now. I was going to be entering motherhood without him as he focused on his health. It was the most important decision of my life to go through with my move to California. I had to escape the memories of pain from my past if I was going to face this new pain. I needed a space of clarity, and being by the ocean is just what I needed to bring myself closer to God as I endured.

I came to learn a few things about myself but even more about God and His love. God is so good. How can I say that when some would feel He was being so unjust in my life at the moment? Well, God loves to shine bright in dark spaces. There were many ups and downs through my pregnancy, and most were mental. I ended up experiencing a deep depression that only grew deeper once the baby arrived. Postpartum depression was not a place I thought I would be, but through this pain, one thing remained...God's constant love.

I never once felt absolutely alone, because anytime I started to feel the tug of loneliness, God would always send a comforting feeling over me, letting me know I was not alone in this. I felt the will to persevere, because I felt that from this dark place, God would still shine through and help me see the blessings. He seemed to always be present in sunsets, deep prayer, new friends, family from back home, and in desperate moments when I felt most alone. I truly feel that love is absolutely everything. Through the darkness the father of my child was going through, I knew that all I could do is love him through it. He is now in a better place with his health, and we are enjoying the sweet moments with our little one.

I have experienced much heartbreak in my life, and God's love is what powered me through each one, teaching me to rely on His grace and love in order to grow from the pain that life throws at us. I know that life will have its dark moments, but I don't know when they will come. I can be sure to never give up on my journey as a mother and friend because God will always give me the strength I need to persevere. After all, God is love, and love is everything.

To find out more about Ana Maria and her journey go to:

https://www.avidahermosa.com

Love

.

Chapter 7

A Battle Within

Self-love is a battle that has taken me a long time to win. I have always had confidence in who I am as a person, because I live by the values that my parents raised me with, and they are the most amazing people I know. But I had an ongoing battle on the inside that I needed to overcome.

Who I was and what I saw in the mirror were two different things. I think I have now come to terms with the fact that I had body-image issues. I never saw myself as skinny enough or in shape enough, even at ninety-three pounds, which is the thinnest I have ever been. I was watching Dr. Phil, and an anorexic woman was standing in front of the mirror. He asked her what she saw. She described the fat on her arms and hips, and I began to cry. She was skin and bones and practically dying, and she still couldn't see it. I wanted to scream at her, "What are you doing? Your family needs you. You are killing yourself!" But then I instantly felt ashamed, because I knew exactly why she felt that way. I had felt the same way about my own body. I saw every flaw, and even when I was skinny in every sense of the word, I still couldn't see that I was. I saw a girl with chubby arms and legs, and I would hide my arms, afraid that people would laugh at me. I never took extremes like that woman did to lose weight, but I knew exactly how she felt. It's the loneliest most hopeless and lost feeling in the world.

I can't tell you the exact moment in my life when those types of thoughts started popping up in my mind, but I can tell you why. Just look around at the women in magazines, movies, TV shows, social media, and of course, some of the biggest influences in music. They all fit a very specific mold of beauty that is packaged to perfection. It is very hard to live up to. As I have gotten older I realize that a lot of that is airbrushing, posing, and tricks of the light. But growing up, you just see it and try to be like it as much as you can. So many young women these days are affected by body-image issues, and strive to be perfect, that they often lose their self-esteem and then themselves.

I could have been consumed by that feeling but I wouldn't allow myself to go there. I was good at hiding it and I kept those feelings locked away inside. Instead of becoming emotional, I took to the practical part of it. Losing weight was just something that I needed to do if I was going to a successful singer. I had made the decision to be an artist at nine years old, when most kids were deciding what doll they would play with, or what outfit they were going to wear. I knew even then that my path was going to be toward something big, and it was going to take a lot of hard work to get there. I had a reason to change, and I found the strength within myself to beat that little voice that told me that I was fat and wouldn't be who I wanted to be.

I didn't always worry about my weight. It all started with a hormone imbalance that triggered polycystic ovarian syndrome. Due to its symptoms they got me started on medication really young. The medication for it caused me to gain some weight and then I ate to make myself feel better—and gained more weight. It was only for a short period of time. But after that, I was never as thin as I felt that I should be. At the most I was 120 pounds, which is still nothing at all. But that was what my mother weighed at the time and it humiliated me to be the same size as her. I felt defeated and devastated. She was thin. And she worked hard to stay that way. But in my mind, she wasn't supposed to be like me when we were that far apart in age. Plus, she was my mother. I would cry, and she would candidly tell me, "Well, if you want to be an artist, you need to lose weight." She was always supportive and caring but made it very clear that that's all there was to it. I was in a business that required me to be skinny. And I knew that if I wanted to be successful, I was going to have to work hard and project the image that they expected. So I did what I needed to do.

For me the answer was simple, summer camp. I begged and begged to go to camp—and I ended up going. It was actually a weight-loss camp. I was embarrassed, so I never told anyone. But I wanted to be there so desperately. I begged for an answer to fix this fat blob that I saw in the mirror. I stayed for a month in this beautiful place. When I got there and looked around I felt confused. Although I saw myself as fat and out of shape in my own mind I didn't look like any of the other girls. Some girls could barely walk. They hobbled up the stairs, barely able to breathe because they were so overweight.

I was the same size as the leaders or even less. According to them I had a few pounds to lose to get to my target weight, but I was by no means fat in any way, shape, or form. But yet, when I looked in the mirror, a chubby girl was all I saw and I felt like I needed to be at this camp.

By the time I left I had never been so fit or tan in my life. We would wake up in the morning and have to walk a mile. Then we would eat a very healthy breakfast spend the morning in exercise class, and then have a light lunch. There would be an evening dance class of some kind mixed in with another class of yoga, and then a very healthy dinner. We would also have a fun activity like watching a movie to wind down the day.

Every day was like that. I had never worked out like that, so it was new for me. I loved it! I actually had a great time. I went to the beach and the amusement park and made some pretty cool friends. The most important thing that I learned was what it took to be healthy. I had never really thought about it until then. I just ate what I ate. And I ate pretty healthy for the most part, but I never took an active role in my health that way before. Overall, I think it was a very positive experience, but at that time, other kids my age wouldn't have understood it. So that secret has stayed with me until now.

After I got back from camp, I worked even harder. I had a

trainer who helped me with my diet and exercise. I remember one time that she told me if I stood with my feet together and there was no space between my thighs I wasn't working hard enough. I also worked with a choreographer for three hours, three times a week. Plus I had singing lessons and I was going to high school. I had a very busy but exciting life. I enjoyed staying busy plus it kept me away from the high school drama. I devoted my life to music. And my drive just pushed me harder. I never gave up. On top of a full schedule I would go to the studio to write and record, which was my favorite thing to do. And then I performed on the weekends. I was on radio shows that were heard all around the country and I participated in doing in-store promotions where I would sign autographs while they played my music in the store, which was really cool. It made it a lot easier to sell records that's for sure. It was hard work but so much fun! I loved taking pics with the fans. But one thing that I always remembered is that it's a business, and a tough one at that.

I can remember this incident as clear as day: I was seventeen years old, and I was headed in to do a photo shoot with a very prominent photographer in the modeling industry. I can still recall the feeling. I was nervous, and I could feel the excitement welling up inside me as I approached the door. A man opened it, and he sized me up instantly. He looked at me from head to toe and mumbled something as my mom and I walked in. The room was in this huge warehouse in Oakland, California, and it had been transformed into a photography studio. The walls were huge windows, and the sun was shining like diamond rainbows through the little squares that created the perfect lighting. The room was warm and inviting, unlike him.

I thanked the photographer immediately for the opportunity to work with him, and he very curtly asked what I was going to wear. I had decided on a purple jumpsuit, and I was ready to put all my modeling classes to the test. I no sooner walked in wearing the outfit than he took one look at me and said, "When you lose ten pounds, come back, and then I will do the photo shoot."

All of my insecurities came rushing back. At this point, I was 110 pounds soaking wet, and any other person would have looked at him like he was crazy. But I politely said, "Yes, sir. I will be back soon." And I got to work. I knew what was required of me, so I did it.

Three weeks later, I returned at a hundred pounds and had the most incredible photo shoot. That's how this industry is. And if you want to be a part of it, you just have to realize what sacrifices you are willing to make.

It's funny, but now that I have given up the idea I had created in my mind of what it was like to be an artist like Shania Twain, Carrie Underwood, Britney Spears, or Beyoncé, I have become so confident in who I am. I am what I call a "profectionist"—a word that I have created. It means "a professional perfectionist." I am so hard on myself about everything. If it's not perfect, it will not see the light of day. Period.

I know what it takes to be in this industry at that level, and I knew then I wasn't ready. Now that I am, I am on a new journey in my music career in a very different way. And I am so excited for this new chapter as an author, songwriter, singer and single mother.

I am thankful for it all. Even though it's caused me to fight many battles within my own mind and heart, it has also caused me to never give up on myself which has made me stronger than I have ever imagined. I have worked on my self-esteem and self-perception issues and have a newfound confidence. I have chosen to live a new life and I have won the fight. I can now look in the mirror and see what is actually there—not a distorted perception of it. Now I am nowhere near as skinny as I was, and I don't know if I will ever be again, but I finally feel happy with what I see. My hips are a little fuller and my legs and waist are a little thicker, but I finally feel beautiful and sexy in the skin that I'm in, and I love the gift that God has given me. My body is His temple.

We are all beautiful in our own ways.

"Be kind, for everyone you meet is fighting a battle"

-Plato

Life Story by Jax Young

My name is Jax Young. I go by Cowboy Jax. I was born in Evansville, Indiana but grew up in a lot of different places. I always like to say that I'm a gypsy soul that saw the world through a windshield. When I was younger, I lived in South Georgia and in multiple other places in Georgia. I went to thirteen different elementary schools growing up. That was in the late '80s early '90s and certain times in life were very difficult because my mother was bipolar type II. There really wasn't a lot of concentration on mental health during that period so my mom went undiagnosed for some time.

My childhood was pretty intense because of my mother's mental state and at certain times we all experienced physical and mental abuse due to her toxic relationships. Certain circumstances happened in Georgia which prompted my grandmother on my mother's side, whom I call my "Nanny", to step in and keep me from going to a boys' home permanently. With that one action she changed the path of my life.

The habits I formed while growing up as a street kid and being the only white kid in deep-south ghettos were very traumatic and impactful and affected me greatly. Coming from ghettos in Georgia and then moving to small-town America where there was maybe one stoplight in the whole town, was a culture shock. I immediately got mixed up with the wrong crowd and started doing what I knew to do to survive on the streets. I sold drugs, got into fights at school, hung out with the wrong people, and made the wrong decisions from the time I was in junior high 'til I was a junior in high school. My principal said that I would either be dead or in prison by the time I was 25.

When I was 17 years old and in my junior year of high school, a girl I knew was killed in a car wreck. It really hit me hard how fragile life is. That was the first time any kind of impact like that had happened to me. I realized we are not bulletproof. And the way that I was leading my life at the time was not the best path. The first of many changes in my life began to happen after that.

My military career came into fruition when I was 18 years old because of my Pawpaw. That's what I call my grandpa on my mother's side. My maternal grandparents were a big influence in my life because my mom was in and out of the picture. I never really had a father figure growing up. I like to say I am a self-made man. But the one father-figure that was in my life part time was my Granddad. He saw that I was into a lot of bad things and he saw that my life was going downhill pretty fast so he told me I was going to join the military, so I did. I had just turned 18 when he took me to the recruiter's office and I signed up to join the United States Army.

My mentality was "If I'm going to go, I'm going all in." I wanted to be in the Infantry and be in combat and possibly go to Ranger School. After I completed basic training and AIT, I pursued the Green to Gold program where I could become an officer and become a JAG lawyer. My lifelong ambition at that time was to become a U.S. Supreme Court Justice. I was actively pursuing that when September 11th, 2001 happened. I elected to go back to active duty after 9/11 because at that time we had no idea what was going on. All we knew was that the United States had been attacked and that there was going to be retaliation from this side and we didn't know where or how the war was going to happen. I could not foresee myself staying in school with all this going on. Plus I had little brothers so I thought if I went, they wouldn't have to go. I left college and I left all my ambition of being a lawyer to go back to active duty. I was stationed at Fort Campbell, Kentucky 101st Airborne Division 1st of the 502nd Infantry "Air Assault."

During my time there I met a fellow soldier, or what I like to call my battle buddy Rel Ravago, IV. He was from Southern California. We hit it off pretty well. I used to sing in the platoon command post (CP) all the time which was our meeting area where we would clean our weapons. I was stationed at Fort Campbell so when we had leave, we'd come down to Nashville to blow off some steam. One night when we were downtown Nashville, Rel asked me to get up on stage and sing a song. I said I'm definitely not going to do that because I really didn't know about karaoke at that time. Well he convinced me and I got up and I sang. It was well received and so around the whole base, or at least our Battalion, I was known as a singer. More accurately, I had sung - I wouldn't necessarily call me a singer at that time. I didn't really know a lot about country music to be honest with you. I knew that there was a thing called the Grand Ole Opry but at the time I never knew the significance of Nashville, Tennessee.

One thing I have learned in my life is, I was born to be a soldier. Although I didn't know it for sure until I became one. Life comes at you fast and gets you when you least expect it. Everything changed for me during a combat training exercise. I was heading up to the third story of a building on a ladder in the dark when I got hit by a can of S.A.W. ammo that came out of a sack. It hit me right in the face and ended my military career. I went 15 years with a traumatic brain injury; although I didn't know that until recently. Three weeks after I had gotten out of the military my unit deployed to Iraq; which was not too long after I had been forced to leave due to my injury. Tragically, my battle buddy Rel was killed in action in Iraqi Freedom in 2003. I found out through 'People Magazine' that's how he was killed.

For some reason after I found out Rel was gone there was something that inspired me to want to truly become part of the music industry. There was a contest called the Colgate Country Music Showdown and to enter, I needed to have a demo to turn in. I didn't know anything about demos so I went to a local studio and went to cut a demo. The studio heard something they liked. I spent the next two years writing the first songs I would ever write and putting together the first album I would ever be a part of. That eventually is what led me to Nashville, Tennessee to pursue professional music.

Now I've been in the Nashville area for almost 11 years. Being in Nashville has been a journey for me in a lot of different ways. Over the course of the years that I've been in this town I've had many opportunities to appear in front of the camera and behind the scenes and also focus in other areas in professional entertainment by singing and songwriting, ballroom dancing, acting, modeling, all of those different kinds of things.

One of the events at which I performed was a show in Kokomo, Indiana. The show was a benefit for two soldiers. One was a paraplegic from the Marine Corps and the other had been wounded 37 times in a combat fight in Afghanistan. The town of Kokomo had come together to raise funds for these folks through a motorcycle club called the Asphalt Templars. Everything I have done with my music career, other than probably one show, always had some kind of driven cause or purpose behind it. I didn't intend for it to be my business model but it just happened that way. I was doing a benefit concert and what I found out was there were charitable organizations out there whose policy was to donate less than half of the money raised to help veterans and their issues. I was determined to change that.

This was my first time being exposed to the power of charitable corporations and basically what I wanted to do was to use my artistry combined with charity to create an Iron Man Strong Tour and create a grant fund in each state and use the money raised in that state to help those in need. It led to me working with some really cool people in the music industry, most notably Johnny Neel from The Allman Brothers, who is a number-one songwriter. He's done a tremendous number of different things including winning the Lifetime Grammy Achievement Award. He was my music producer. There were also other amazing people who were involved and invested in what I was doing as well. Basically through the process of creating it I fell on hard times and the bottom fell out of everything that I was doing. I ended up homeless.

It all really came to a head when I attempted to take my life. It made sense. I had gone 38 years of life round-for-round never sitting out one round. Never giving myself a break, and never letting go of the things that I should have let go of. Never saying, I'm defeated but I'll get back up. So when you fight for that long you are running on empty at some point, why wouldn't suicide be *an option?*

The day I went to kill myself I had an argument with my now estranged wife and I went up to my son's room (he wasn't home at the time). I locked the door. And I attempted to hang myself with a belt. I don't want to say I got lucky but I believe that God stepped in. I was fairly asphyxiated which means the lack of oxygen to my brain was very thin so I had almost accomplished my goal. I thought I was dead. I took the belt off from around my neck and thought, God, is this Heaven? Is this hell? Where am I at?

I walked over to the door and opened it. I thought, well I guess ghosts can open doors. I walked to the steps and decided I was gonna have some fun with this. I figured I am a ghost so I'm just going see if I can float down the steps. But when I stepped off I started falling. I had what I call the 10 second epiphany. It took about 10 seconds or what felt like 10 seconds for me to hit the ground. In that moment I realized I wasn't dead. I could have been dead. My neck could have been broken. It took just a few seconds, but I clung to life. I begged God to please let me live. When I hit the ground I felt pain surge through my whole body; my shoulder, my neck, my ribs. I had never rejoiced in pain so much in my life. I was alive!

That day I disassembled suicide because what made suicide so romantic was number one: if I kill myself, everyone's life would get better. If I murdered myself, everyone's life would be more enriched. That wasn't true because I saw the level of guilt and responsibility felt on my estranged wife's face. And number two: it's not your life to take. If I truly wanted to die then when I was falling I would have just said let's get it over with. But I clung to life, because it's not my life to take. From that point forward I had no suicidal thoughts because I killed the romance of it. The other thing that I figure out in that process was that there's no such thing as suicide prevention. I had gone through multiple counseling sessions at the VA. I had been behind the doors in the green pajamas at the VA in the mental health ward for 3 days. And yet I still attempted to take my life. So I really focused on my counseling because I really needed to understand what this was about. In that journey I learned that we need more anxiety education in this country.

Anxiety tells you "immediate thought, immediate action". If you read about people that attempted to take their life and weren't successful they will tell you the first thing they felt afterwards was immediate regret for attempting suicide. I didn't want to pull the trigger. I shouldn't have jumped off the bridge. I shouldn't have kicked the chair out from under me. The reason why is because when that impulsive thought subsides, which is temporary and impulsive the "fight or flight mechanism" in your brain engages. Fight or flights says "I will fight to live or I will flee" so in that immediate moment you're clinging to life because that's your natural instinct. Suicide is based on a temporary impulse. Not a natural instinct. No matter what the circumstances are.

At this point in my life it all came full circle. Everything that I had gone through from being injured in the military, to Rel getting killed in Iraq, to going through the struggles and tribulations that I went through for those 15 years with traumatic brain injury and almost ending my life, it all came together and finally made sense. I understood they were all key elements in helping me understand what Save Home Front, this 501(c)(3) registered non-profit I had a vision for when I was homeless, was going to be about. I reached out to someone I had met in a private organization I am a part of and told them what I was thinking about. They were on board and I had 8 weeks to create this non-profit that I had envisioned in my mind and get it off the ground.

*Once I made the choice to start Save Home Front I immediately began to take a difficult journey. I went to 30 counseling sessions with the VA and started traveling around the country and connecting with Community neighbors. What I found was that Save Home Front needed to be a help up not a hand out for Veterans. That the accountability needed to be on the Veterans and that the narrative needed to change. Less than 1 percent of the country serves, and 99% of the country supports. But they don't really understand each other, other than what the media puts out there. Save Home Front has two main goals. One is to offer "**a help up, not a hand out**" system through our unique programs for Veterans. And the second is to create a positive media message for the 99% who support our country and the 1% who serve our country to make up 100% of America.*

When I think of the words never give up, I guess for me I think common sense. The reason why I think that is because I ultimately gave up. I was willing to cash in the most valuable commodity: myself. You are the most valuable commodity on this planet. So what do you have to lose in going for anything in life? If nothing else, we always stand to gain. You need to rejoice in your trials and tribulations. And understand God's plan in its full validity. No one is ever going to be able to give you the answer to why anything has ever happened to you. You can be influenced or inspired but no one is ever going to be able to make you do anything. You are always going to gain something by never giving up. Whether that's knowledge, reward, sadness, or emotional value. Life by definition literally means to never give up. As long as you are living, as long as your brain works, as long as your heart beats, you have a responsibility to yourself to never give up.

*I have a wake-up seminar. It's called "Life After Suicide - Killing the Old Me." I'm cool with motivational speaking but what I'm doing is **not** motivational speaking I'm here to wake you up. That's why I call it a wake-up seminar. There is a core value that I discuss called PATH. A lot of people talk about preordained destiny, fate, or coincidence. But what I have learned in my experiences is that life comes down to four things:*

1. *Pain.*
2. *Anxiety*
3. *Tolerance*
4. *Health*

Pain - Understanding and identifying your pain is essential because your pain will always teach you something if you afford it that opportunity.

Anxiety - We all have different levels of anxiety. But you need to understand what anxiety is and become educated about it and how your mind literally deals with it.

Tolerance - Once you manage your anxiety and understand your pain, that knowledge is going to gauge the tolerance in your life. Becoming numb is just as dangerous as giving in to all of your anxiety and fears. You need to be able to have that gauge of balance and tolerance of the different things in your life because that's really going to decipher the final outcome.

Health - Your physical and mental health is a combination of your pain, anxiety and tolerance.

The PATH of your life is most important. Wherever you are in the spectrum of how you feel on a daily basis, moment by moment is what really helps you to define your life.

We live in what I often call delusions of grandeur. We push pain to the side as much as we can because everyone wants to look shiny and new. Everyone wants to be presented without flaws. I say embrace your flaws. Embrace your pain. Embrace your anxiety. You have no idea what's going to happen in the next moment so you need to stay present in the moment. You have to set goals for yourself. It is very important that you understand what it is to go from point A to point B to point C because success isn't something that is made of luck or wishes. Success is something that is made of doing things on purpose, embracing failure and never giving up.

To find more information about Save Home Front and to download the song

"Leave A Light On" go to:

http://www.shfveterans.org

Chapter 8

Attitude and Gratitude

In life there are pivotal moments that happen to us that shape the life we create. They can be brought about in so many different ways such as meeting people, life changing experiences, self discovery, education, or even combinations of some or all of these. No matter how they happen once they do, they end up guiding us on our journey and completely design the path that we set for ourselves. This is not easy to do because you have to be brutally honest with yourself and the experiences that you have had. But once you embrace this idea and you understand these concepts, it will help you to understand who you are and why your life is the way it is.

Dr. Phil says that there are certain defining moments that make you who you are. *"According to Dr. Phil, you can trace who you've become in this life to three types of external factors: 10 defining moments, seven critical choices, and five pivotal people. But first it's important to understand the following terms:*

Ten Defining Moments: In every person's life, there have been moments, both positive and negative, that have defined and redefined who you are. Those events entered your consciousness with such power that they changed the very core of who and what you thought you were. A part of you was changed by those events, and caused you to define yourself, to some degree by your experience of that event.

Seven Critical Choices: There are a surprisingly small number of choices that rise to the level of life-changing ones. Critical choices are those that have changed your life, positively or negatively, and are major factors in determining who and what you will become. They are the choices that have affected your life up to today, and have set you on a path.

Five Pivotal People: These are the people who have left indelible impressions on your concept of self, and therefore, the life you live. They may be family members, friends or co-workers, and their influences can be either positive or negative. They are people who can determine whether you live consistently with your authentic self, or instead live a counterfeit life controlled by a fictional self that has crowded out who you really are. "

https://www.drphil.com/advice/defining-your-external-factors/

I encourage you now to take a look at your own life and make your own list.

For me there are two major life defining moments that can I think of, that have affected my life greatly. Karaoke is first because that's where this whole musical performing artist journey started for me. Karaoke has affected my life greatly at two different times and both experiences set the trajectory for my life in two very different ways.

The first life defining experience happened to me the first time I ever got on stage. It was mid afternoon and there were maybe around 8 people in a smoky Mexican restaurant in Pleasant Hill, California. This was not just any Mexican restaurant. This was the kind that on your birthday they set a huge sombrero on your head and the staff would come out and sing while taking a Polaroid to document your humiliation or pride, depending on how you felt about being the center of attention. At this point California hadn't banned smoking inside yet and the smell of cigarettes hung in the air which I knew well because my next door neighbor smoked like a chimney and the smell would linger whenever she was around. The other one was strong, pungent and yet foreign to my young senses.

Now thinking back I can say with almost certainty it was alcohol due to the environment I was in but at the point it was just another distraction as I made my way to the stage. My dad dared me to get up and sing. I couldn't have been more than 5 years old but I actually can remember it clearly; which is why it is one of my top defining life moments. It was terrifying and fun all at the same time. The song started and I belted out each note of "Oh Donna," my favorite song by Ritchie Valens. I loved every moment of it. As I got off the stage filled with pride and excitement, I ran back to my parents. I got a big high five from dad and all I kept thinking about was what I was going to do with my huge winning prize of $20.

Another memory with karaoke that set me on the path that brought me right to where I am today happened in downtown Antioch, CA. A few years after taking singing lessons and performing around town my dad discovered a new Italian restaurant with a karaoke bar called "Il Giardino." It was my favorite karaoke place. I wasn't supposed to be there past a certain time, but people loved to hear the little girl with the big voice sing, so the owner and my parents always let me stay out way past curfew. It was a dream come true for an eleven-year-old girl who wanted to stay out late on a school night.

In California where I grew up, country music was not popular at all. Bone Thugs-N-Harmony and 2Pac filled the radio airwaves. TLC, Aaliyah, Boyz II Men, and Mary J. Blige were all over MTV, and oldies were the only songs on my dad's radio. One night a boy and girl came in and started singing a new type of music that I had never heard before. The instrumentation was filled with fiddles instead of synthesizers, and the steel guitar replaced the electric guitar. The bass beats that were normally the driving force became a distant memory, replaced with waltzes and honky-tonk rhythms. The lyrical content was stories of heartbreak and cheating and losing and finding love. I was hooked. I was entranced by the melodies, and I wanted more.

I learned about my soon to be favorite country singer, Patsy Cline, when I bought my karaoke machine and the enclosed karaoke tape of the song "Crazy." The emotional journey of the melodic piano intro and the vocal inflections spoke of pain. At eleven years old, I didn't know anything about love, yet even then I knew exactly what she was singing about. At this point, though, I was still influenced by my friends and surroundings, so country music didn't find its way into my musical journey until I began to write songs on my own a few short years later.

I loved to write, so I wrote and wrote and kept telling myself, "I am going to write a pop song." But nothing ever came out sounding the way I planned. The pop sound that I wanted was just not there. It was pure country. The lyrics, the melodies, and the stories just resonated loudly I AM COUNTRY MUSIC. So at that moment my life changed. I looked up and said, "Okay, God, if this is what you want me to do. Let's do this." I made the decision right then and there that I was going to be a country artist. So I gave it my all and never looked back.

I joined the Northern California Songwriters Association and took a songwriting class from Steve Seskin, who has hit songs such as, "Don't Laugh At Me," "Grown Men Don't Cry," and "Life's A Dance." He taught me the techniques of what it takes to craft a song. He also produced my first professional demo. That demo fell into the hands of Scott Haugen who was a representative for Jerry Crutchfield in Nashville. Jerry Crutchfield was a major influence in country music. He was a producer for many hit records. Jerry established MCA music as a major publishing house signing many hit writers, as well as serving as Executive Vice President of Capitol Records for 4 years. He even worked with Elvis Presley. He mentored me and took me under his wing producing another demo and soon I was sitting in front of major record labels in Nashville. That experience is what eventually led to my move to Nashville in 2003.

In Nashville I learned that even though I haven't done all I plan to do yet, I have what it takes to make it. I have been close to a record deal several times. The first time was when I was working with Jerry. Sony Records was interested in signing me. I also got offered a management deal with PLA Media and was being scouted by Curb Records. But things don't always happen as planned. I was on tour in Europe when I was notified that Curb Records wanted to sign me to a record deal but by the time I returned they had already signed someone else. The final time was after doing a showcase for Lyric Street Records I was told they wanted to sign me only to find out that Disney shut them down a couple weeks later.

The music business is exciting and heartbreaking all at the same time. The music business has its highs and lows and you never quite know when, how, or where the right opportunity will come. The only thing that you have to do is be prepared for when the right opportunity arrives. Some may seem like great opportunities at the time but if they don't happen it just wasn't meant for you. And that's not to say that it won't happen, it just wasn't the right opportunity. That's not only in the music business but life in general. Doors will always open, but you have to be ready for the right one at the right time. And be thankful for every experience you have because it prepares you for every step forward that you take.

The second one is my biggest, greatest, and most life changing and defining moment ever. As I have been in the process of writing this book I have found the grandest expression of love that I could ever have been given. I am so happy and thankful to say "I am pregnant." 5 weeks to be exact. If you had told me a year ago that I would be writing those words I would have told you, you were out of your mind. I have always had issues with my menstrual cycle, and was told when I was very young that I had polycystic ovarian syndrome so having a baby was going to be a long disappointing and difficult process should I even try it. I also have had a very strong career path that I have followed since I was 9 years old when I told my Mom that music was my life; and a baby was not part of that vision. I was always told by every record executive to remain single and baby free.

Well here we are now and I just took the pregnancy test and after 3 different tests and a blood test at the doctor's office I am proud to say I am going to be a Mommy. I am so excited to be on this new journey of life. I must admit that I am terrified and excited and happy and nervous, and all of those emotions of the not knowing what happens next. But I know that God is watching over us and he will take care of me and this amazing blessing that I have growing inside me. Each day I will pray this prayer as I move through this journey of love that God has put us both on.

Heavenly Father, I know this precious little baby comes from You. I thank You for this miracle growing inside me and for giving this little baby to me as a gift, but also as a gift for the world. I can't wait to see the amazing plans You have for this child.

I ask You, Father to watch over this little blessing each day as my baby continues to grow. I ask that You will sustain me in good health and surround me with your love throughout this whole pregnancy.

Thank You for this amazing miracle.

In Jesus' name. Amen."

"Life is 10% what happens to you and 90% how you react to it"

-Charles R. Swindoll

Life story by Jayce Hein

My name is Jayce Hein. I grew up in a town called Middlefield that's literally in the middle of a field. I'm not Amish, but there were Amish all around me. It was kind of cool and like a third-world settlement.

Music was always a huge part of my life because my dad was a singer and songwriter. He played guitar and everything. He moved to Nashville in the early sixties, had a publishing deal, and wrote some stuff back in his day. He was a great, amazing singer too. So I was always around it. He always had a band. And then my older brother was also in a band. He's about ten years older. When I was a preteen, thirteen, whatever, I started playing. I always went to their band practices and stuff. My aunt and uncle were in the band too. They'd play out at one or two shows a week.

My family was very musical, and I always wanted to do it too. My plan was that after high school, I would move to Nashville, but instead, I had a kid and got married. Then I got divorced and decided to make the move in 2007. I had a friend who played in a band; her name was Jessica Homolish (now Jessica Miller). She was from Ohio, like two towns away from where I grew up, but then she got signed to Warner Brothers.

When she moved to Nashville and got married, she and her husband kept talking to me about moving. When I finally did, they were gracious enough to let me stay with them for three or four weeks until I could get a job and a place. For the first two years, I worked during the day, going out at night to watch and absorb everything. I went to writer's nights, different shows, and just tried to meet people and find out how it worked—how songs worked, *how they were put together, and how people created them.*

It was kind of cool to hear the writer's perspective on the songs that you've heard on the radio. It was fascinating and made me want to write music even more. I started writing a lot in 2009. I got my first cut on the Jason Aldean album the following year, which was just crazy, and life changing. That album launched him into superstardom, playing stadiums and stuff. It was cool to be a part of that. It was a lot of work to get there, but it was worth it. I signed my first publishing deal that same year in 2010. I've written full time since.

I should say that my whole life, I was kind of overweight, and it played into my music career. You know how it is. Everybody says, "You've got to look the part and act the part." They don't care—you could be the most amazing singer in the world, but if you don't look the part, then you usually don't get the part.

So I always struggled with that. I had a lot of stuff going on in my life, which is not an excuse, but I was addicted to food, and it got it out of control. Big Vinny, my piano player, had done Biggest Loser a few years back. In 2013, he called and said, "Man, the producers from the Biggest Loser contacted me and said they're looking for someone in the music industry for a show called Extreme Weight Loss. I told them about you. I hope you don't mind. You're in if you want it."

This freaked me out, but I agreed to take a week and just go talk to them. I finally got it out of my head that it was a bad thing and realized just how good it could be—not only for losing weight, but you never know what could happen with TV and stuff, being put out there in front of a large audience. Anything could happen. So, it was good all around for me to do that. It was a win-win. That was the hardest year of my life. It took so much work. I ended up losing 180 pounds, which is crazy. That's like an entire grown man.

It was a lot of hard work in an eleven-month period, but it was all worth it. I would do it again in a heartbeat, even though a lot of it sucked. There were a lot of fun times, but it wasn't fun most of the time. But we had a lot of support, not just from Chris and Heidi, the trainers on the show, but also from other castmates and our families. My family is extremely supportive. I had a little boy—well, he's not little anymore. At thirteen years old, he's taller than me now. It's really scary—I feel like he should still be this little kid. Anyway, that was the hardest year of my life, but it was also the greatest year of my life.

I gained so much confidence, and I started playing out. I almost signed a record deal at one point. It didn't end up happening, but it was close. Everything, I think, works out the way it's supposed to. I'm glad that it didn't happen, because I don't like being on the road constantly. It isn't my cup of tea. But it was cool to be able to do that, and the show really pushed my whole music thing. They got me out there, and they had me playing in front of the audience on TV and stuff, so that was very cool.

Growing up, you always hear, "You can do anything you put your mind to." I don't know, I guess I've always been one of those people. If you put something in front of me and tell me I can't do it, I'll go out and do it. I know that's kind of cliché. A lot of people say that. In music, there are always negative people who say you'll never be successful, trying to crush your dreams. I had that a lot in my life, and it just made me want success more. Moving to Nashville and having some success was very rewarding because it was something people always said would never happen.

With the weight-loss thing, it was the same. Everybody assumes that overweight people are just lazy. People don't understand that it takes a lot to get that way. Nobody chooses it. Consider a hard-core heroin addiction, or whatever it is. People don't want to be that way. You don't want to be overweight, but you get to that point, and then you don't know how to go back.

My success with the weight loss was really amazing too. I loved being able to get out there in front of three million, eight million—however many people watched the show, and show them that it's possible for you to reach their dreams, whether it's music or weight loss. I went from 424 pounds—which is unbelievable to think about...it just freaks me out now—to 220 at the end of the show, I believe.

It was just a (literally) huge difference. I feel like too many *people don't realize that they can chase after something and accomplish it. Too many people think that they can't. They think that things are impossible, but they're really not. I'm just a nobody from Middlefield, Ohio, and I had some crazy stuff happen in my life that shouldn't have. It's just weird. But it proves that anybody can do it, if they go out there and work at it.*

I love that—never give up. At one point, I was told that ABC wasn't sure about me for the weight-loss show. They wanted to get some more film, so they put together this music show for me to do at the Listening Room. At my second song, Chris showed up and surprised me, saying, "We choose you to be on the show, blah, blah, blah." I bawled. They show that on TV, and it's so funny, because I tell everybody it wasn't happy tears. That was me freaking out. Like, Sh*t, I do not want this. I didn't want to disappoint anybody, or especially Big Vinny. I knew how badly he wanted me to do it, because he cared.

My son, who was nine or ten at the time, came onstage and gave me a hug. He said, "You deserve this, Dad." When he said that, it just clicked, like a light went on in my head. I was like, I do! Why can't I do this? I do deserve it. Never give up. But it took a ten-year-old child to remind me that I couldn't give up. I had to go for it. It was the opportunity of a lifetime—not only to change my life, but others' lives.

It's amazing. I still get messages from people in different countries, like Argentina and Egypt, because it still airs all over the world. They're seeing it for the first time, three years later. They tell me, "I watched your show two months ago, and I've lost forty-five pounds now."

A lot of people are against the reality-TV weight-loss thing. I see a lot of hate, like, "You shouldn't put them out there. You shouldn't make them so vulnerable by making them take their shirts off onstage." Well I'm glad they did that, because it shows viewers that we're just regular people. We were just regular, massively overweight people, just like a lot at home who are watching the show and need some kind of inspiration.

Unfortunately, not everybody gets the opportunity that we did, so their opportunity not to give up and to keep moving forward is inspired by our episodes and seeing and believing, "Wow, look what we can do."

It just blew me away that my son just said, "You deserve this, Dad," on his own. He wasn't prompted; he just thought of that. And they played it in my episode like ten or twelve times. It was funny, I had probably thousands of comments that all said, "You deserve this, you deserve this." After the show, it was cool that they took what he said and just kept using it.

For the show, we had to run like crazy, do Iron Mans, mud challenges, different 5Ks and crazy obstacle things. We were doing things that fit people do, and all of us were fat. Every time I wanted to give up and be like, "Screw this," I had like a tape in my head that kept playing those words: "You deserve this, Dad." That's what kept me going. It was that and the fear—when I first went on the show, they said, "If you don't do something about this, you probably have three, four, maybe five years, because you're going to die of a heart attack."

You always know that in the back of your mind, but you never really face it until the doctor says it. You know it's not scripted for the show; it's just her talking to you behind closed doors with no cameras. And you're like, "Oh, sh*t. I better get in shape." It kind of motivates you too.

It doesn't matter...I always said with the show, if you can change one or two lives, it's worth it. Every one after the first one is a bonus.

It's amazing, because at some point, somebody changed our life, and we have to pay it forward.

Chapter 9

Life Is a Race

Life is a collection of moments. That's it. It's thousands of short perfect and imperfect moments that make up our day to day life, and together they create long-lasting impressions of who we are and who we become.

You are in control, and you decide where your life is going to go. These words are so powerful because it's not just an emotion but it's an action that's attached to an emotion. When we realize what we are supposed to do in life, then action has to come next. Otherwise, it's still just a dream. The minute action takes place; it's no longer a dream. It's reality, and you are pushing it into existence.

You don't have to start with a big step. It may just be waking up a little earlier and having a healthy breakfast, or it may be running five minutes to build up your stamina for a bigger run in the future. It could be relocating for a position you really want, going that extra mile that you know will pay off. It could be something bigger, like fighting cancer, where every step that you take is another battle won.

We all have moments when we need to be strong for ourselves and the people we care about. For me, that journey started when I met my friend Cynthia Tieck also known as Cindy. She had been diagnosed with a disease called scleroderma, a chronic, connective-tissue autoimmune disease. Currently there is no cure for it. According to the National Scleroderma website, "The word "scleroderma" comes from two Greek words: "sclero" meaning hard, and "derma" meaning skin." In this disease, the body overproduces collagen, and it can affect different parts of the body. It affects over three hundred thousand people in the United States alone.

When I met Cindy, she had been told that she had a very short time to live, but that didn't scare her, not for one second. She is one of the most amazing women I have ever met. There's not one topic that she doesn't know something about. Her passion for life and helping people is an important part of who she is. Her ability to overcome anything tough in her life is inspiring. She does this with incredible passion and grace. In getting to know her, I have seen the true definition of strength. There were days when she didn't want to get up because of the pain, but she always did, and with a smile on her face. She had trouble swallowing, and cold would cause her pain. She was taking tons of medication to help get her through the phases of the disease, but you would never know it. She was always out and about, making the world a better and safer place, especially in our neighborhood and for others who were diagnosed with scleroderma.

As I got to know Cindy, I went on the scleroderma journey with her. After watching her as she went through the phases of scleroderma I got inspired to write a song called, "Right There." This song is so important to me because of how much it means to her. When I sent it to her, she fell in love with it, saying that it told her story. That meant everything to me, because as a songwriter, that's my biggest goal—to tell the right story that has the truest and most important message that can be created with powerful words and a harmonious melody. She loved the song so much that she sent it to the National Scleroderma Foundation. They loved it and invited me to perform it at their National Convention in Boston. That was such an incredible honor.

I met a wonderful man at the National Scleroderma convention named Erion Moore II and here is his inspirational story.

We all have our reasons to never give up. My reason was to be the man my grandmother raised, inspired, and wanted to see.

Before being diagnosed with Scleroderma, a rare chronic-progressive autoimmune disease, I was on the path to completing that process. I was known to my friends, teammates, and co-workers, as a young man that worked hard along with good work ethics. So when the symptoms of my disease started I couldn't understand why people who were consistently around me did not believe when I said something was wrong.

Growing up I played sports and there is always that determination attitude to be better than the next or the best. Play until the game is over. I had a coach who would never let you short cut or end abruptly. It was just another reason to feel giving up is not an option. Leading up to my senior year of college I worked with both juvenile and adult offenders. I enjoyed walking around the neighborhood and cleaning in and around my home. People around me knew this and commended me on being a busy and active person. They also knew they could always count on my help if they needed assistance. Then something hit me. At 23 years old I wasn't sure what was going on with my body. My hands and endurance along with fatigue were some of the symptoms that dramatically affected me. It was subtle yet noticeable. I would tell co-workers, classmates, teammates, and friends that I just can't keep up like I used to. Unfortunately, some took it as "senior-itis" or being lazy. I could probably understand that type of talk and treatment from people who never knew me, but not from anyone who knew me personally. Why would people think I'm lazy all of the sudden? I had never been this way.

Over the next few years my health deteriorated rapidly. My body wouldn't recover as quick as it used to as I was often tired and sore, and I felt like I couldn't loosen up my muscles or skin.

I went from 6'6' 205 lbs to 130 lbs and needed assistance and wheelchairs or walkers to get around. However, I wouldn't let that stop me from being the same person people knew before the condition. I was staying active to prevent more joint damage and contractions, traveling back home for visits with friends and family, laughing and basically making sure nothing changed. This is when people would compliment me on keeping a smile through this period of my life. Often I would hear how they couldn't stay positive or being impressed that this disease was not bringing me into depression. Hearing these statements and talking to my grandmother almost daily gave me more of a drive to never quit. My thinking was, if people are relying on me for whatever reason - whether it's comfort or inspiration and such then why should I give up. They need me! Not sure if it was true, but I used it as motivation.

A few years after the disability became so severe; I needed to be at home with nurses. There was a point where I said, okay, this may be it. I did not want to die in a long prolonged death. Luckily, I found the stem cell transplant as an option to save my life. After doing some research and talking to medical assistants at the hospital, it was no doubt that this was the only option for me. The support from everyone was astonishing. People were asking how they could help. Some helped by coming to visit, offering donations or just being there if I needed someone to talk to. At this point I was 29 years old and ready to start another chapter in my life. The transplant was going to be rough, but it was the best way to end my 20's, and move into my 30's. However, to my surprise, there were no side effects during the procedure and people were amazed that I took it as if I were just getting my blood drawn. The procedure worked immediately and I already started to contemplate my future wants and needs. People would say "man, you just had a life saving procedure and you're already looking to get back into the normal adult routine." Now everyone else started to realize that I was still a hard worker and had the drive to be the best I could be. This started to bring in more admiration and appreciation. Here is another reason I couldn't quit - proving the people wrong who said that I was being lazy. It was already enough that they saw me at my worst, but I had to show that my disability did not change the person I was. My grandmother was very excited about my future, probably more than I was. She already had plans of what I was going to do, where I would live, and who I would be with if I had let her decide.

Following the transplant, things started changing for the better. I wanted to prove to myself and everyone else that this was not going to get me down. As my health started to improve everyone around me loved that each week I made plans to be active and set long term goals. Scleroderma patients that have been in my same shoes always see me as motivation, and I like to make sure people *know that even with a potential fatal or disabling disease, that there is or can be hope many times, especially in regards to the medical advances in society.*

At this point when people say "You're an inspiration," "Love to see you still fighting" or "I was going to stop this or that, but thought of you." Hearing these compliments keeps me motivated and asking myself, "How can I quit with so much support?" I feel great when I hear those inspirational quotes. And I am so thankful to everyone. It's statements like those and the support that they give me every day that make it hard to quit. At this point there is a feeling "I have come this far. No reason to stop now." Even more so, I feel you either deal with it (adapt) and it can get better. You just need to work on it. Now at 35 years old, life is better than it's ever been. I am looking forward to the future and I am using my experience to help lift up others that feel they are in a hopeless position and motivate them and support them the way that others have motivated me. This is my story and it's just the beginning. I have a lot to add to this world and this is why I will never give up.

It is so wonderful to meet so many incredible people from all over the world who are all fighting this horrible disease and have been inspired by my song. Music is so powerful. The messages that I got were truly incredible. Here are a few that I would like to share with you:

"Hi Angela. Your song is wonderful. Bless you for bringing awareness to this disease. I was diagnosed about three years ago with it. I am a single mom of a four-year-old son whom I love and cherish. It gets a little challenging day to day with raising him and dealing with the disease but I keep my head held high and keep moving forward. You are such a beautiful person inside and out and thank you again for your kindness and helping us to shine the light on this disease to others."

*

"That song "Right There" is really good. Thank you for

your help in our hope to find a cure. I'm 22 and have been dealing with it since 15 and have lost four fingers from it so I really like your song thank you."

*

"Angela what a beautiful song, "Right There." My mom passed away from Scleroderma about eight years ago and was a journey of struggle with her in the illness. I listened to this song and cried because it is hard every day for those who live with this illness and their families and this is such an inspirational song. I will definitely pass along to some others. What a beautiful thing to do - thank you for requesting me as your friend I needed to hear this song, I felt close to my mom again."

Across the country there are annual walk-a-thon fundraisers for local Scleroderma Chapters. Every step that is taken is to raise money to help find a cure and do research and education about the disease. The walk is filled with the patients as well as the support teams that help them fight this debilitating disease. Everyone wears shirts to represent their teams, and everyone walks with a fighting spirit that is undeniable. It also gives a special day to honor those who have passed away from scleroderma as well. Every day, we get closer to finding a cure for this disease. I know that we will never give up, and with time, we will see the answer "Right There."

National Scleroderma Foundation Website

http://www.scleroderma.org/

"The race of life is a marathon, not a sprint"

-Tony Robbins

Life Story by Jerrod Kerr

My name is Jerrod Kerr, and I'm from Pennsylvania. In 2014, I was working in the natural-gas industry, in the oil fields of South Texas. On my way to work, I went through a construction zone, and my truck rolled. I was ejected. I broke my back at the thoracic vertebra T10 and was paralyzed from the waist down. I had no feeling or movement.

My life was completely changed, and I had to relearn everything from scratch. But that's sort of the beginning of the end of the story.

Growing up in Pennsylvania, I played ice hockey and got a degree in mechanical engineering from Penn State University. I worked in Texas and Louisiana for about ten years. Prior to breaking my back, I had life pretty much figured out. As I saw it then, I was successful in all the life areas—you know, my relationships with my family were good; I had a support system of a lot of friends in Louisiana, where I was living at the time. I had a great job making great money, a couple hundred grand a year. I had my own little consulting company, so I got to pretty much choose my own schedule. I worked two weeks on and two off. The two weeks I was on, I was doing real manly work and got to use my brain. It was a great job, and I got to be a leader in that space.

I had had this plan that in three years, I would retire from that job and do something completely different, where I felt like I was giving more back to the world than I was receiving. When I broke my back, I was about six months into the plan, so I was devastated.

I knew that if I was going to survive, it would take something extraordinary, centering around not giving up and not quitting on myself or the people around me.

I was in excruciating pain when I came to in the hospital, and my blood pressure was erratic. It would go through the roof and then drop, and then it would do that again. They wouldn't give me anything strong for the pain and I just wanted it to go away.

I would get these shocks, like a bolt of lightning going through the legs that I couldn't even feel. It was kind of like ghost pains, real sharp and excruciating. One moment, I was in tears, the next moment in lots of pain, and then back to tears. Coming out of that space, I had a coworker with me. I just knew that if I was going to make it and have any kind of progress physically, I was going to have to make some difficult decisions. I had to choose the best spinal-cord injury doctor. One was in Denver, and the other one was in Miami, Florida. So I got on a plane heading to Miami.

In Miami, I began my rehab. I had another back surgery, where they removed some bone fragments that were impinging on the cord. The doctor told me that one day, with technology the way it is, I would walk again, but I would have to stay healthy. And I didn't know how long the wait would be, so I set out on a mission.

When I was first able to sit up, I passed out from vertigo. There are these things called tilt tables that bring you up slowly until the point where you can sit up, slowly and gradually, your body and your brain can adjust to that. I had to rely on people to go to the bathroom, to shower and clean, and to turn my body so I wouldn't get pressure sores at night. In rehab, I just decided that I was going to get up every day. I had to create a powerful contest— that was one of the keys to never giving up. What I mean by a powerful contest is that if wasn't worth getting up and getting out of bed, if it wasn't a big-enough gain, then what was the point? Why get up? If I was just getting up and out of bed in the morning for myself, it wasn't really worth living for. It wasn't worth going through that level of pain and discomfort and the challenge of not being able to experience the lower half of your body the way you used to. So I had to create a great game.

The contest at first was, *All right, there are about twenty other people in this rehab facility with spinal-cord injuries. All of them have days when they just stay in bed all day and don't do their rehab. So I decided that I was going to rehab every day, no matter what, even if I didn't want to. No matter how much pain I was in, no matter what transpired—whether I had an accident and went to the bathroom on myself, or if I didn't think the nurses were doing their jobs properly, or if I had a bad attitude. Whatever! I was getting out of bed every day. That went on for a week or so. I thought that doing that would affect somebody else so that they got out of bed every day, no matter what.*

There was a twenty-one-year-old Mexican man who had fallen off a roof, and he didn't have any family here. I began to feel grateful for having a support system large enough that I was getting cards in the mail. I had a brother fairly close by who came to see me. I had friends fly in to support me and even stay in the hospital with me. So, I thought, I have to give this back. I made sure the young man got up every day and did his rehab, whether he felt like it or not.

From there, the next contest was about the therapists. Most were phenomenal and excellent people that you just wanted to be around. Some had bad days and were human, complaining about things that were really ridiculous from my point of view. You know, like, Oh, your feet hurt? I don't want to hear about that, you know? Get over yourself already. I can't feel my feet, let alone have the experience of having them hurt! And so, I created the game of, "I'm going to make a difference with them and have them find a place to be grateful for that day and have fun at their job. Let them see that they are making a difference by helping me and these other people"—whether those other people said so or not. I wanted to leave people with the experience of being empowered and that the world is worth contributing to. The world is worth becoming someone who is powerful in the face of any circumstance. From there, holding on to the hope of walking again versus accepting not walking right then, or feeling my body, was like a dichotomy. And I don't think that hope was a powerful context. Sometimes it was just necessary to get through certain things.

With hope, hopelessness can also arise, and that just didn't serve me. Hope wasn't powerful enough to keep me moving forward. I had suicidal thoughts a lot, but one of the main things with that is that I would talk about it. It didn't always land well, but I didn't sugarcoat it and try to make life seem better than it was. I would just tell my brother, "Look, I'm worried about offing myself. Why stay here? What's the point? This is ridiculous. I'm in incredible pain every day, and they tell me this is it. I've pretty much plateaued. It's not going to get any better without drugging myself." And I was committed to not using Percocet and getting off medication after I got out of the hospital—and I did.

The next project I created was about this exoskeleton contraption. You sit up in it and strap it onto your legs. Somebody pushes a button for you, and the machine stands you up. It has a gyroscope on each side, and when you shift your weight from one side to the other, it causes the one mechanical foot to go forward, and so on with each shift. It takes something to get moving.

Well, I created the possibility of having that contraption available for people in outpatient therapy at Health South in Sunrise, Florida. I was just unstoppable. I rolled into the vice-president's office without an appointment, and I told her that there's a contraption out there called the Re-Walk System, and I could see that its company was committed to people with spinal-cord injuries having a great life and being supported, having the best therapy in this particular facility. I told her that was one of the reasons that I was in Florida—I had flown there from Louisiana and saw the contraption as another way to market the facility, besides giving people the opportunity to walk again who hadn't had that experience in years. She liked the idea, and we got in touch with the people from the Re-Walk Company and Channel 10 News, and we created a story around it to bring awareness.

That was a big-enough game to keep me engaged and moving forward. Lo and behold, once a month, they brought the Re-Walk System into clinics, plus a couple of therapists at Health South who were trained in getting people up and moving on the system. As a result, two people have bought systems to use at home. They're very expensive. I thought, "Now what?" So I created another game, which was to get these things approved by the insurance companies. Yeah, I can go and raise money and buy one for myself, and that would be great, but what about the rest of the world?

How can I impact the rest of the world so that other people in my situation who don't have a voice, who don't think they have a voice, who don't have the means to go out and just buy one of these things, how do we get one for them so that they're empowered and have a semblance of a life the way it was before? I'm now in an appeal process with my insurance company for one of these, and I have some lawyers on my side. And once a precedent is set, it will open the door for other people.

So, really, I think the powerful contest is what's gotten me through. I've had moments when I cry. My brother, who's five years older than me, had concerns about whether he could take care of me. As he was getting me to the front door at home, I fell backward. You have to pop a wheelie to get over the curb. He caught me at the last second before my head smacked on the ground. The chair went flying out from under me, my legs flopping around. And he started crying, and I was like, "Hey, whoa, we're not dead. We're good! Get me up, get me off the ground." And he did, and we got inside. A month later, he had another breakdown getting me into the bed. I couldn't even transfer myself from my chair to another object without help, another seat, or another bed. Slowly, I worked up the muscles to do that.

Some days, I would look down at my legs, that had deteriorated from what they used to be and cry. Because I worked out a lot, I used to have strong legs like tree trunks. I had to buy baggy pants because my legs wouldn't fit into regular ones, they were that stout. And now I'm looking down at these legs and they were floppy like an old man's in his eighties or nineties with muscle atrophy and loose skin just hanging off his bones.

I would grieve and cry over my loss over what it was to be this thirty-two-year-old male. But I didn't stay stuck. To get more into the emotional side of things, I don't know how else to describe it other than that lying in bed, there was anger, there was possibility, there was resentment, there was resignation.

But I would put on YouTube videos and watch motivational speakers. One of my favorites is C. T. Fletcher. He's a body builder, and he cusses a lot. It was like I was just stepping into this space of getting angry at some moments and being like an egomaniac. Whatever it took to just get through it—"I'm going to make it, because I said so, and because I can—or die trying." And so, that was a powerful contest—to get up, to work out, to get to rehab, and to stand back up.

When never giving up enters my mind, I think of a friend of mine who passed away of a heart attack when he was twenty-five. I played ice hockey with him in Pennsylvania. I was a pallbearer at his funeral, and two other pallbearers died within a year. It took years for his mother to become functional again in society. His mother sent me this plaque that Darren had. It said, "NEVER, NEVER, NEVER GIVE UP." To say that I never gave up is sort of misleading, because I gave up lots of times—but I didn't stay there. I give up a lot, even today. But the difference is that I look at what I can create to get moving again.

When I wake up in the morning, there's one guy on my shoulder telling me to hit the snooze button, roll over, and go back to sleep, and then there's the other guy who says, "No, you're not done yet, you're not done yet. Get up and make a difference. Get up and see what you can contribute." And so, I found that the power really is in serving others—not like I'm being Mister Noble or Mister Selfless or a martyr, by any means, but that I get fed by serving other people. I get fed and energized, and I get the energy to make a difference, to go through my day—to have a day, not to be resigned about life but to be empowered with life by serving other people and looking to see if I can be a contribution, living each day as it may be the last. If this really is it, there are no do-overs.

Chapter 10

If You Dream It, You Can Do It

Every day that I get up I am living the dream. I get to wake up in Nashville, the country music capital of the world. I get to eat, sleep, and breathe music. It's everywhere. It's in the grocery stores, restaurants, malls, even on the streets. It's not just the music that makes Nashville great, but the people that live here.

Nashville is an amazing place, not only because of music but also the music history that's ingrained in every part of the city. Nashville is the dream. People come here from all over the world to follow their destiny. But it's not easy. So many people focus on the "I have to be a superstar" mentality and "If I'm not there yet, then I am a failure." You can't think that way about anything in life. It will make you feel sad and depressed and then you really won't do anything productive. Instead, you have to be grateful for each moment that you get. And live in it. Enjoy the ups and the downs of each experience, and learn from every moment, good or bad.

I have been so blessed to be able to do the things that I have done. Sometimes I think it's important to reflect back on your positive experiences, especially during tough times. When you struggle it's easy to get lost in all the frustration and forget all you have accomplished. I have learned that if I allow myself to embrace what I have accomplished and be proud of my own success in those hard moments, it makes everything easier to tolerate and overcome.

I have had so many incredible experiences in this amazing life so far. And I am so thankful. I have gotten to go backstage at the Grand Ole Opry, Sing the National Anthem for NASCAR and for the Golden State Warriors. I got the honor to travel to England, Norway, the Azores, Italy, Turkey, and Japan to entertain our men and women in uniform who keep this country safe every single day. I got to hear my songs played on the radio and do radio interviews across the country, be an extra on the *Nashville* TV show, act in commercials and music videos—mine and others', including one of my favorite singers, Martina McBride; and step into the doors of the biggest record labels in Nashville and showcase my talent.

It's exciting and fun but things are not always great one hundred percent of the time. And we just have to accept that. We all have ups and downs. You can feel higher than the sky almost like you can touch the stars and then fall straight down and feel lower than you ever imagined and that's a scary feeling. But you can't let that discourage you. You just have to enjoy every moment as it comes.

I believe that everything that happens in life, good, bad, or indifferent leads us to be right where we are meant to be at this very moment. I have had such an amazing, frustrating, exciting, confusing, scary, happy life that has been full of hard lessons, and I am thankful for all of it because it has taken me on this amazing journey to find myself. I finally feel like I know what I am supposed to be doing, and that is more satisfying then I can ever describe.

One of the lessons that my dad taught me very early on is that if you commit to something you need to follow through with it. Period—no matter what else comes up that might seem more appealing at the time. I have lived by that, and I always will. My dad and mom have shown by example what they want and expect from me. I feel so blessed to be able to live my life the way I do every day. I am living the dream. It's not exactly the one that I pictured in my mind, but this one is even better than I imagined.

After all of my life experiences, I am now at a place where I truly realize the power of music. I knew that music was powerful and great and that it made people feel things. But there's so much more. It has the power to teach us, guide us, and bring us together in a way I never imagined. I am going to use the gift that God has given me to inspire us all, to make us stronger, more tolerant, and empathetic and to be able to relate to one another, knowing that we all have the same moments and feelings that change our lives. We all have trials in life that don't go exactly how we planned, but that's okay. It's in those moments of heartache that we find where our heart truly belongs.

I am finally at such a place of peace in my life. I always dreamed that I would get to do music for a living, and now I am. It wasn't in the way that I had originally pictured where I was traveling 365 days out of the year from country to country and being on top of the *Billboard* charts, but I am okay with that. I am now focusing on making music that has a positive meaning, that I can share that with the world in my own way. And that means more to me than anything.

I don't know what the future holds for me, but that's what makes life so exciting. I used to be so afraid of the unknown, but now I embrace it. Because it's in those moments that our destiny is shaped.

I am just getting started, and I will never give up!

"If you can dream it, you can do it"

-Walt Disney

Life story by Ricky Mena

The difference between being successful and being unsuccessful is having the self-discipline necessary to resist the lure of the excuses.

I dreamed that my grandmother who had passed away came to me and showed me a movie where Spider-Man was visiting children in hospitals, spreading joy and presents to thousands who needed it. When I asked her what it had to do with me, she said, "That is you, and when you wake up, you'll do that." I literally woke up. My first Spider-Man suit arrived in October of 2014, and a few days later, I made my first visit. Since then, I've seen over ten thousand kids in need all across America.

Our little ones are the future. They are full of life, dreams, imagination, and wonder. I constantly walk into rooms and lives that may have a dark cloud looming above. My one wish is to shed some light—to dive headfirst into the world of fantasy via my superhero suit, to leave bits and pieces of inspiration, courage, bravery, and encouragement that are the very staples of my true, personal self. You see, the image of Spider-Man is just a key to a door that allows me to tap into their hearts and boost belief, hope, and faith. I may walk in as Spidey, but I leave them with my own heart, passion, and spark to live. They may never know who I really am beneath this mask, but if in some miraculous way, the happiness I bring them allows them to know more life, more love, and more strength, then my name is irrelevant in comparison to the message I deliver.

Trials and tribulations mold who we are. They humble our hearts and minds while igniting our spirits. They let all of us know that life is hard. Nothing is ever easy. And we have to work the hardest for the things that hold the most value. No, not material value, because how valuable is anything that depreciates over time? How valuable is something that can be taken from you? The value I'm talking about is within: perception, love, personal growth and evolution, heart, friendship, strength, and meaning. No one can take those treasures from you, and it's what you do with those gems that will further solidify who you are in this world and life.

Most dreams in today's world fall apart, fail, and wither away because far too many people are afraid of giving something the world may view as farfetched. Maybe you don't give yourself enough credit due to lack of confidence. Maybe you lack the inspiration or the fire while giving in to excuses because it's the "safer" or "easier" choice. Regardless of what your goals are, getting your results won't be easy. That's something you have to come to terms with. If your excuse is "It's too hard," then it's safe to say that as long as you think that, you will not be a success in the realm of what you're trying to accomplish.

Now, take a deep breath before you get defensive, and listen. I've met thousands of children who fight cancer daily and go through the hardest days any of us have ever seen. They don't have the option of saying, "This is too hard, so today I'll take a break." I've seen moms and dads break down in tears yet still push forward because "too hard" isn't an excuse to give up. I've seen single mothers of several children, people missing limbs, folks with disabilities and more hit the gym every...single...day because they chose not to make an excuse, and that's what separates them from the pack.

So I'm sorry, but in my shoes, I can't hear you when you say it's "too hard." You have to stand up when it hurts, fight when you're weak, go harder when you're tired, and give it your all when you're on empty if you want to be the difference in this world and make a change in your life. Wake up every day and get up, no matter how bad it hurts, and chase your dreams down as if you couldn't breathe without them.

Dedication, consistency, and persistence are the will to keep going, regardless of outcomes both good and bad, while never being content with a loss or a win, because the act of running as hard as you can is where you derive your purpose to exist. Cry because you're strong, embrace pain because it's the only path to your growth. Accept change and follow the gravitational pull of your own evolution. It's looking in the face of everyone and everything that challenges you and running right through them like a wall made of papier-mâché. It's having faith when you're at rock bottom. It's believing when no one else does, harnessing your drive when exhausted, having determination at your weakest moment, and showing resiliency when you're broken. It's choosing to work and practice over sleeping or partying. It requires incredible sacrifice. It's having an unwavering commitment to the discipline necessary to accomplish every goal on your list. I am the change I want to see in the world. "Are you?"

There are times in life when we feel defeated, times when it feels like the very sky we held up came crashing down atop our shoulders. It's normal to feel overwhelmed by the mountain of obstacles life sets at your feet. It's in those moments that we are forged by the pressure bestowed upon us. The cold, dark, seemingly bottomless abyss of our unknown future during those specific times gives us an opportunity. It gives us reason to be strong. It guides our faith in an upward direction. It anchors our belief in overcoming the impossible, because we absolutely have no other choice. History will remember us for our victories, but we are most certainly defined by our ability to lose and continue on. To be relentlessly resilient is to live fearlessly in the darkest times, gazing off into the candlelit hope in the distance.

If you hold a tear with your hands, you'll find it almost has no weight. If you hold it with your heart, it can weigh you down. All of my experiences thus far have taught me so much. I rise every morning with an ambitious drive that is unexplainably strong. It doesn't let me rest too long. It doesn't let me sleep too much. It keeps my feet moving when my body, mind, and heart are exhausted.

There are days when I wake up and the first thing I do is cry. I open my eyes, and it just hurts to breathe because of how much pain and suffering I've seen in children over the last few years.

There are days when I have to force myself up and say out loud, "Get up, Ricky. Keep going, Ricky. Never give up. You're not done, Ricky." Over ten thousand kids are locked in the vault of my brain as memories, and it all translates into feelings inside of my heart. I'm often asked what gets me through. How do I keep on going? How do I handle all of the hurt? It's the hugs, the smiles, the tears of joy, the overwhelmingly happy children who felt like their hero wasn't too busy for them. It's the moms, dads, brothers, sisters, and all the others who write me the most heart-wrenching thank-you messages explaining how much just being there meant. It's the pictures of memories we helped create that immortalize loved ones for family members after some children unfortunately pass away. It's love, it's passion; it's heart, God, and caring all wrapped in one.

So, even though it hurts to take steps forward sometimes, it would slowly kill me to stop, knowing what a difference I could make but am passing up. I believe it's this way because I feel I can help this world, but even more powerful, God knows I can too and helps me do just that. My little angels in heaven are working. God is working. I don't know why I can literally feel the world's pain, happiness, sorrows, and euphoria, but I thank God I can. I thank God for making it impossible to stop, because with my life, I will make a difference so big, it will echo long after I'm gone. Let us love more, as we were intended to do. Let it start with me—and make sure it doesn't end with you.

This isn't a dream anymore. It's real, and I'm ready to change this world for the better! Thank you God. Thank you, all of you, for your support, and thank you to my team, family, and friends.

To find more information about Ricky Mena and Heart of a Hero go to:

https://www.heartofahero.org/

If You Dream It, You Can Do It

Chapter 11

Breathe

Breathe. I love this word because it's so simple, and yet it is everything in life. Like the Faith Hill song says, "Just Breathe." Breathing in and out every day is something we all do every day. And it's needed to survive. I believe that oftentimes, we take it for granted. We don't treat it like it's something special, because it just happens. But if we stop and think for a moment and realize everything that takes place when we take a single breath, it's absolutely incredible.

The National Heart, Lung, and Blood Institute tells us this is what happens when you inhale. "When you breathe in, or inhale, your diaphragm contracts (tightens) and moves downward. This increases the space in your chest cavity, into which your lungs expand. The intercostal muscles between your ribs also help enlarge the chest cavity. They contract to pull your rib cage both upward and outward when you inhale. As your lungs expand, air is sucked in through your nose or mouth. The air travels down your windpipe and into your lungs. After passing through your bronchial tubes, the air finally reaches and enters the alveoli (air sacs). Through the very thin walls of the alveoli, oxygen from the air passes to the surrounding capillaries (blood vessels). A red blood-cell protein called hemoglobin (HEE-muh-glow-bin) helps move oxygen from the air sacs to the blood. At the same time, carbon dioxide moves from the capillaries into the air sacs. The gas has traveled in the bloodstream from the right side of the heart through the pulmonary artery. Oxygen-rich blood from the lungs is carried through a network of capillaries to the pulmonary vein. This vein delivers oxygen-rich blood to the left side of the heart. The left side of the heart pumps blood to the rest of the body. There, the oxygen in the blood moves from blood vessels into surrounding tissues."

And that, my friend, is just when you breathe in. The human body does amazing things.

I know how important it is to breathe, because there was a time in my life when I wasn't able to. Those were the scariest minutes of my life. Now I know this is going to sound funny...but I almost drowned at swimming lessons. I was pretty young, but I can remember the moment vividly. We all have moments that get ingrained in our minds, and this is one of those for me.

I was five years old and doing great in my swimming class. I was feeling confident and on top of the world. I kicked by the side of the pool like my life depended on it. Little did I know that this was going to be truer than I could imagine. I was following directions as we moved on to the next challenge my teacher had in store for us: the kickboard. A kickboard looked like fun, and I got on one with ease. My arms gripped the board with confidence as I glided like a swan across the water.

Okay that's an overstatement, but let's just say I looked like I knew what I was doing. And I wasn't the only one. The swimming instructor was so confident in my ability that he decided to let me continue to go across the water without him. And instead of waiting for me he went back and got the next kid to bring across.

As I kicked my feet wildly I drifted toward the deep end on my way across the pool; although that really wasn't a concern to me. What mattered more was that I was making my way across this large swimming pool. When I did I felt so happy. Now those who have been on a kickboard know this, but it is something I didn't realize at five years old—a kickboard is all about balance. I felt pretty confident at this point and decided that I would get off this rubbery tomb stone shaped contraption as easily as I had gotten on. Well it happened, but not in the way I wanted.

As I reached to grab the edge of the pool for my victory, my hand slipped off the side as if it were glass, and me and the kickboard flipped like a pancake on a hot, greased pan. I lost complete grip of the board and went straight to the bottom like a dead weight. I felt my lungs fill with water, and it hurt to breathe. I was drowning. My teacher quickly dove to the bottom of the pool and pulled me out. My eyes burned from the chlorine and my stomach felt nauseous from being so scared. After throwing up a bunch of water, it had never felt so good to feel the air in my lungs. I was alive.

I am so thankful that in the midst of all the chaos my teacher realized quickly I was underwater and went quickly from being my teacher to my hero. He truly saved my life that day.

I am telling you this story because even though I was so young it was such a big lesson that I learned that day. Life is never promised. And we have to live every moment of it. From that moment I've never taken a breath without realizing that there is a chance that I might not take another. Taking a breath is an amazing gift, and we need to be thankful for it every single day.

"Breathe. You're going to be okay. Breathe and remember that you've been in this place before. You've been this uncomfortable and anxious and scared, and you've survived. Breathe and know that you can survive this, too. These feelings can't break you. They're painful and debilitating, but you can sit with them and eventually they will pass. Maybe not immediately, but sometime soon, they are going to fade and when they do, you'll look back at this moment and laugh for having doubted your resilience. I know it feels unbearable right now, but keep breathing, again and again. This will pass. I promise it will pass."

-Danielle Koepke

Life story by Paula Smith

I woke up this morning feeling grateful to be alive. I walked outside and felt the cold, brisk air hit my face. I took a deep breath and looked up and smiled at the sunny blue skies. I thought, Today is going to be a great day. Life is something I don't take for granted anymore. In fact, before I go to bed each night and when I wake up each day, I thank my Heavenly Father for allowing me another day to live and thank him for answering my prayers. I dare not skip a day to thank my Heavenly Father each night and day, for it is he who has helped me deal with my past and present tragedies and the sickness that I have experienced in my fifty-nine years of life. Do I have stories to share!

I truly believe that life's tragedies are life's lessons. And with our life's lessons, we are then able to help others who are going through turmoil in their lives, whether it is physical, mental, or emotional abuse or maybe dealing with an illness alone, or someone who is too scared to talk with others about it. I wasn't always this open about my life. In fact, I was very secretive about what happened to me when I was seventeen years old. It's only been a few years since I have truly opened up about my childhood, which has shocked my friends and my immediate family, because they see me as happy and bubbly. But I found that it was therapeutic for me to share my secret.

Without going into much detail, as it is too painful to write, the secret that I carried for the past forty-two years is that my father attempted to kill me by choking me and throwing me down the stairs. Yes, I had counseling, and, yes, I was happy the day my father died at the age of fifty-four from lung cancer. When I went to visit my father at the hospital a few days before he died, he was in a deep sleep. When my mother left the room, he woke up, looked right at me, and said, "Paula, I still hate you." And he went back to sleep. Those were his last words to me.

Now, I could have allowed his words and the pain of what he tried to do to me eat at me, and I could have fallen victim to depression, drugs, and alcohol, but I refused to let that happen. Why? Because then, my dad would have won. He would have loved that. So I made the decision the day of his funeral, which was on Valentine's Day, that I would love myself, that I was worthy, that I would be a survivor and not a victim—that when I had children, I would love them more than ever. I can't even recollect one time my dad uttering the words that he loved me. He was a very rich and powerful man, but he did have a horrible childhood, as he was an orphan who later in life became a very successful businessman, owning several successful businesses. It wasn't that he didn't know how to love or be affectionate, because he was very affectionate and loving to my other sisters.

He saw me as strong and aggressive, not fearing him, which would set him off. But when he was choking me, I didn't fight him. I just lay there letting him choke me. It was my brother who saved me. After my father's death, the nightmares of him coming after me were intense and frequent. They lasted for decades.

I realized that for me to move forward in my life, I had to forgive my dad, which was certainly very difficult to do. Once I did that, the nightmares ended. So, always remember to forgive someone who has hurt you. You don't have to forget it, but you must forgive in order to move on with your life. The way my father treated me made me determined to be the best mother I could be to *my children. I breathe and live for them. They inspire me, they motivate me, and they love me. I couldn't be happier.*

Now, that wasn't all that happened to me. I have experienced one near-death situation after another. It's almost laughable. But I survived them all, and I am thankful. I have survived car accidents and illnesses, one drowning and a near drowning, several head injuries (one resulted in a brain injury that caused me to lose my taste and smell), and several tumors throughout my body that are, thankfully, benign. I was bitten by a brown recluse twenty-eight times, lost six pints of blood because of aspirin. I've had breast-cancer scares and skin-cancer scares. The list goes on and on.

With each accident and illness, I have always remained positive, never fearing I would die; nor did I wish for sympathy. I never allowed the word "fear" into my vocabulary. I look at each episode as another day in the life of Paula. After what my dad did to me, everything else became small. Nothing, and I mean nothing, can bring me down, because I am a fighter.

God kept me alive when my father tried to take my life away by sending my brother. He still keeps me alive, as I know he has a bigger plan for me. What it is, I don't know. Therefore, my life experiences, whether good or bad, have inspired me to share with others that this, too, will pass. Yes, it is okay to be scared. Yes, it is okay to cry. Yes, it is okay to be mad. But at the end of the day, you have to snap out of it and decide if you wish to stay in this dark hole or be a survivor and dance in the sun. I choose to dance in the sun.

Ask yourself: "Is my life really bad compared to others?" Helping others or volunteering to help others is the best self-medication. If that means calling and checking on someone, then make that call. If it means posting an inspirational quote on Facebook, then by all means, post it. You'd be surprised at the number of people who will appreciate it and thank you for it. There is too much to live for to allow the past to keep you from taking that breath of fresh air and enjoying life.

We don't have a lot of time here on earth, so make the best of it and be happy. Inspiring others is the best medicine you can offer. It doesn't cost a dime to buy happiness. The only person you can change is you. Be that person and never let anyone suck the life out of you. God gave you life, so enjoy waking up every morning. Walk outside and say, "I thank God for giving me the air to breathe."

Whenever you do not understand what's happening in your life, just close your eyes, take a deep breath and say, 'God, I know it is your plan. Just help me through it.'

Breathe

Chapter 12

86,400 Seconds

Making choices is probably the most important thing that we do in our lives. We make them every single day. Whether we are deciding what to eat, what to wear, and even how to feel, choices affect every aspect of our lives. Decisions that we make in one moment can affect the rest of our lives.

I was told that our minds can only process one thought at a time, but before I accepted that, I wanted to do my research. At first I was kind of confused, because I thought, well, I know how to multitask (do two things at once). But in reality our brain is just processing one thing after another very quickly. I learned that causing your brain to think a lot and process quickly during multitasking actually can actually drain your energy and make you less efficient at what you are trying to do.

Once I learned this valuable piece of information, I realized something very important: we are in full control of our brain. You have the power. So, how do you want to feel? The choice is yours and no one else's. I think people often get caught up in the idea that someone made them feel bad. They let other people's thoughts or actions affect them. I know I've done that.

I am extremely emotional, which I think in a lot of ways helps me to connect to people through my music and songwriting. I allow myself to be vulnerable, and it affects me. There was a point in my life when I would spiral down...I would have a negative thought, and then that would lead to something else negative, and before I knew it, I was spiraling down like a cyclone. I would get so upset that I would cry and feel bad and not want to talk to anyone. I hated how that felt. I felt lonely, sad, confused, and hopeless.

Then one day, my dad had had enough. He saw me wallowing in self-pity and yelled, "*Stop it!*" I was shocked. I had gotten so caught up in myself and my emotions, that he shocked me right out of my funk.

Then I got angry and was like, "What do you mean? I am supposed to feel bad and sad."

And he said, "No, you are not 'supposed to' feel anything. If you make the choice to feel bad, that's up to you. It's one hundred percent your decision on how you feel." I got frustrated and asked again what he meant. He told me, "You are the one who is control of how you feel. You can choose to either hold on and let it fester inside your heart and bring you down, or you can leave the problem where it's at and not let it affect you, take what you can from it, and move on."

I thought, *Wow, I have that much control?* I felt like I had just become Superwoman and had gained an amazing super power. So I decided to try it out. I had been in a relationship for a very long time and it had really taken a toll on my heart. My partner and I, at this point, were like oil and water. We just couldn't get things to go right, no matter how hard we tried. We had developed such bad habits. Even though we cared for each other, we kept going right back to the same behavior and the same fights over and over again. This inspired my song "Best Fight" and my first music video.

We cared, but it just wasn't working. I had let the problem affect my job, my friendships, my self-esteem, and my overall happiness. One day our usual fight occurred. He would often use the threat of breaking up to control me. He used his manipulative behavior, making a show and threatening to end the relationship as he often did, but instead of falling apart and crying my eyes out, I just left the problem where it was and chose not to let it affect me. I chose to say, "Well, if that's how you really feel, I accept that." I don't have to make it work. And the choice is mine.

From that moment on, I no longer took him back and I accepted that sometimes it just doesn't work. He isn't a bad person, and I wish him the very best. We just weren't good together. This lesson came up again while I was sitting in church this past Sunday. The pastor broke it down very simply: you are in control of your own thoughts. So, the best way to live our lives is to choose to have one good thought and then another and another. Pretty soon, your life will be full of nothing but good thoughts—and in turn, those thoughts will bring you a good life. So, just remember, as you live your life day to day, the choice is yours. You choose to make your destiny and your dreams come true. Never give up!

"There are 86,400 seconds in a day. It's up to you what you to decide to do with them."

-Jim Valvano

Life story by TJ Cates

I'm TJ Cates. I was born in Memphis, Tennessee, at the same hospital that Elvis passed in. When I was a kid, my dad had a grocery store down the street from Graceland, and I would roller skate with Lisa Marie and see Elvis and his friends riding their golf carts around in a big circle. I went to high school with best-selling writer John Grisham. My first acting teacher was Red West who was Elvis' best friend and bodyguard. So I've seen how people born in the same area as me can then just take off to bigger things. And that inspired me.

Where I grew up in Mississippi everyone was a conformist. Everybody has the same belief system. You love Ole Miss, wear khaki pants, red golf shirts, and brown boots and play golf on the weekends. Life is simple and predictable. You vote for the same people, go to the same church and work your typical 9-5 job. But that wasn't me. I always found myself wanting to be different than that.

I was born with artistic roots. My mom is an award-winning published poet and a poet laureate. Since I was raised by a poet, I've always had a creative side.

In the early nineties, I started going to acting classes. My acting coach and I really connected. I've always connected with people doing something outside of the box. As I got more into acting and got an agent, I wasn't getting all the roles that I wanted. So instead of waiting and watching like everybody else sitting there, I would sneak on set. That's how I got some scenes with David Schwimmer and Alan Alda—because I didn't sit in the room with the extras. I went and hung out in the hallway. The director asked, "Are you one of our people?" I said yeah, so they put a briefcase in my hand, and I got to play a lawyer. Meanwhile, everyone else would be like, "Where'd you go the past two hours?" I'd tell them I just got in the movie.

My dad had a grocery store for 30 years and was very successful. We sold it, and what we got for it we reinvested in a new grocery store. But it just didn't make it. It was bad timing, there were big box stores, like Kroger, Costco, and Walmart Superstores across the street from what we were doing. Everybody got excited and liked the well known names they saw in the commercials. Anyway, the family business came to a quiet end. Before that I was president of my neighborhood association, which was 350 homes. Here in Nashville that would be worth half a million to $800,000 per home. We had neighborhood pools; we had fountains and lakes when you pulled in. It was beautiful. It was like West Haven or Franklin. And I had my own business. I had a hummer and a jeep. I had a four wheeler, a boat, and a jet ski. We had everything.

When you don't have a paycheck anymore you have none of that. And it made me realize I'm happier because I'm in an international war film that I was cast in and it's being seen around the world. Even though I was actively getting many Screen Actors Guild (SAG) credits, by age forty, I wasn't getting cast enough to make me happy. So I started learning how to make and edit my own movies, and I cast myself in my own films. I made a few trips to Nashville, Tennessee and found a basement apartment. I had a garage sale bigger than you could have ever imagined in your whole life. I let all my material stuff go, pocketed all that money, and lived on five to ten dollars a day in my apartment.

One of the things that I have learned is that you have to take advantage of every single second of life. It doesn't make any sense if you don't. There are 86,400 seconds in a day. The reason I say seconds instead of minutes or hours is that you can always say, "Well, I've got another minute." But what is really impactful is *hearing how many seconds we have. When you think of it like that it gives you more perspective of how much time you have. "And that's a lot of seconds."*

I wake up and think to myself what are you going to do with your seconds today? "Are you going to answer a phone call, or are you going to sit there and watch TV, or are you going to watch some YouTube video about how to be a better editor? Are you going to go to other entertainment sites to see what's happening outside your little circle?" I do that constantly. Anyone would think this is a sickening work ethic, but I do it all the time, every day. And if I have headphones on, I'm not listening to music. I'm listening to people who are bigger than me and greater than me, pushing me to be bigger.

The biggest thing that I have learned that has served me very well is doing 100 percent of what you say you're going to do. If I'm filming at the Nashville Film Festival on the red carpet, I'm there at 5:30 p.m. filming, because that's when the main people come. By 6:30 or 6:45 p.m., I'm back home at my editing desk, already sharing my interviews.

From the beginning I was drawn to Nashville. I have learned your dream is going to take you places and sometimes it isn't the right places and sometimes you get disappointed and get shot down, but you are making connections and networking if you are smart. And the reason why you ended up in those places to begin with is to make those connections that move you forward. Treat your dreams like a business.

I don't believe in putting vices ahead of your dreams. That's another thing that makes zero sense. I don't expect people to be able to stop them immediately, but what's more important? Which is it—your dreams, or your addictions and destructions? Just let them go.

I always find a niche. I want to see what everybody else is doing and then try to do something different. Or else I am going to look just like everybody else.

I don't believe in setting goals. Let's say that you are running a quarter mile track. You are going to haul you know what to get to that finish line but once you do, what do you do? You slow down. And then get your trophy. Forget that! You can set goals but don't let that be your ending point. You gotta keep going. They say, "Do what is easy and your life will be hard. Do what is hard and your life will become easy." I am not so sure, but take the licks and keep moving forward if you want to experience all of life's possibilities.

Life is about learning. Before we started the Nashville Entertainment Weekly show, I had never edited a TV show before. I knew how to put segments together but I didn't know how to blend a television show together to make sense so I had to go to Google and YouTube to learn. Now I represent Nashville Entertainment Weekly, TJ Cates Productions, and started TJTV. We do sixty minutes of all-original programming a week. We show it in Nashville to two million viewers every Friday night and our numbers just keep increasing. We have definitely grown as a company.

We started Nashville Entertainment Weekly Records, a label that I run with my fiancé Jill Santibanez where we get up and coming artists National FM radio play. We also have Nashville Artist Management, and of course, Nashville Entertainment Weekly. I am so proud of what we have accomplished. Not only have we been Nashville's number-one social-media entertainment show for the past two years, but now we are Nashville's number-one televised entertainment show in our Friday-night 10:00 p.m. time slot. On our shows, we blend Opry stars with the artists that we manage and give lots of opportunities to new and established artists. What I would like to do eventually is take our project to other cities and go nationwide.

As I reflect back, I've been in Nashville almost 5 years and after all this time, I can finally connect all the dots. I thought it was the plan to come here 5 years ago to be a film maker and an actor and star in my own movies and that made me learn the skills about working cameras, getting great audio and making things better with lighting. Those were great tools but it goes further than that. Now because of those skills I have learned I am getting paid to shoot music videos and commercials and am now working in studios where they are making big budget films and Netflix movies and I'm doing my own TV pilot for California on the biggest home network in the country. And that's just the beginning of what I have planned.

If you ask me about why it is that I am successful and continue to thrive in such a competitive industry I would say, I'm steadily learning. That's my gift, never giving up, and never slowing down. My advice to anyone that is looking to be successful in life is to always be learning, and if you don't know about something just research it. You will find your answer. That's the glory of the Internet now.

To find out more about Nashville Entertainment weekly go to:

https://www.facebook.com/NashvilleEntertainmentWeekly/

Chapter 13

Dying To Live

These words are so meaningful in my life because they affected me both literally and figuratively. Literally because it happened on a road, and figuratively because it was a turning point in my life that changed everything about the way I was living and feeling about living.

Now, if you know me, you know that I am **not** an adrenaline junkie. In fact, just the opposite, I am a scaredy-cat with a high affinity for being the queen of NO, turning down every exciting opportunity that comes my direction. Well at least those that involve any level of danger. So this story starts out with one of my less proud moments of giving in to a relationship that I knew probably deep down wouldn't work. We were very different.

We dated, but it ended quickly due to his infidelity. I gave him the benefit of the doubt when he said that he could change, as most of us women do when men are on their knees with tears in their eyes saying "it won't happen again." Very shortly I saw that he had not changed, nor was he ever gonna change. He didn't really want to despite what he said. So we parted ways. Needless to say, he went on to make some very bad decisions and ended up in a very bad place. It was devastating for his family, and since he had moved far away from them, and that made it even harder.

My mom is my best friend and I know that if something ever

happened to me, her heart would be broken in a million pieces—so I am sure his mother felt the same. So me, being a loving Cancer born in the month of July with the typical empathetic personality, my heart ached for her. And when she reached out and asked for help I answered with an open heart. Her question was very simple. Could I get her son's car out of impound and send it back to her?

Now, remember, I said he had been in a bad place. Well, helping his mom with the car was not an easy job to do, but somehow, with the right documents and a mother's prayer, I got it out of impound. I had never driven it before since he bought it after we had broken up, and driving this car was very different than what I was used to. I drove it straight home so that it was ready to go when the shipping company would be there to pick it up two weeks later. When I got home everything was fine. The car sat in front of my house until we were ready to ship it back.

My father called the shipping place the day before to make sure everything was still on schedule, and it was. However, they said to make sure that the car started and could be driven up the ramp, 'cause if it couldn't, it would be another $150 to load it. My dad, being the smart man that he is, suggested that we take the car to get the battery charged so that there would be no issues the following day. The next thing I knew, there I was, sitting once again behind the wheel in this vehicle that was completely foreign to me.

Now I don't know if you've ever experienced a feeling of evil. But let me tell you, I have. I was surrounded by it in that car. As I sat there I had the worst feeling come over me. At this point, for whatever reason, the car would not start anymore on its own, so dad and I had to jump it. We planned to drive around the block to get the battery charged. We were there in front of my house, my dad was facing one way and I was facing the other. The energy around me felt like we were headed two entirely different directions yet not moving at all. I felt an awful feeling come over me, but like most of us do, I tried to ignore it. With each turn of the key nothing happened but a small click followed by the unlocking of the door. It sounded like a gun cocking. *Click, click.*

In the background, I could hear the sound of Bone Thugs-N-Harmony singing, "Ouija are you with me?" on repeat, over and over again. The dark, haunting, chanting voices of Bone Thugs singing, "Mo murda mo, mo murda mo murda me now," in the background in an evil musical round with the words, "Mr. Ouija could you please tell me my future," filling the speakers. I shuddered with fear. I tried to turn it off, but it was impossible. I fumbled with the different buttons and pushed the power button off and on, but nothing happened. Over and over the lyrics played, "Mo murda mo murda come again" haunting me like a ghost. It felt like hours but in actuality, only a few minutes had passed. Once the car finally started, the music just stopped and the stereo shut off. I silently thanked God for that and stepped on the gas to make a U-turn to follow my dad.

We lived in a cul-de-sac, so I had to turn around to get to the exit where my dad was patiently waiting. We lived at the bottom of a very small hill. After you climbed it, you would dip into where the curve of the cul-de-sac began. I had driven it so many times before so it was natural. I knew the speed and the small angles of each turn, and I went on autopilot. Except this time that calm confident feeling I had every time I took that turn was replaced by fear. The brakes on the car were gone. Completely gone! I pushed and pushed hard, but nothing happened. I felt lost. I knew nothing about this car. Not even where the emergency brake was and I could feel it moving faster and faster as we quickly sped toward a house.

I saw my life flash before my eyes. I knew in that moment I had two choices, life or death. Was I going to be weak and go with this car wherever it was going, or was I going to be strong and fight for survival? Now in life, sometimes these decisions are made for you. In my case I believe that angels came and helped me with that decision. And two seconds later I opened the door. I can remember that when I pushed it open it felt like a thousand pounds. And it took every ounce of strength that I had. I pushed it open because every part of me wanted to live. I had so much to live for. Like I said, I'm not a fan of anything dangerous but next thing I knew I was rolling out of a moving vehicle onto the hard concrete pavement. My shoulder hit the ground first, and then the rest of me followed. I felt the stinging burn of the hot pavement as it shredded my shoulder like a cheese grater. Then my head pounded on the pavement and bounced like a basketball. I rolled three times, and my knees and ankle felt the rest of the trauma.

I screamed in terror for my dad to come as I watched the car, that I had just been sitting in, go crashing at full speed into a house. It ran straight into the garage door. The oddest part about the whole thing was that once it hit and went into the house, the garage door had nothing wrong with it but a small curved-up ledge at the bottom. Dad looked everywhere for the car but couldn't find it. He saw that I was still alive and breathing, and although I was covered in blood, he knew I was okay. I told him the car was inside the house, but he didn't understand. The only giveaway was that little ripple at the bottom of the garage door. As he got closer, he could hear the sound of the car still growling softly, so he immediately opened the garage door and shut it off.

The police showed up a little while later and I explained to them what had happened. I got cited for not wearing my seat belt that day, but to be honest, I don't know if I would have been alive to tell this story if I had been wearing it.

Right after the impact of my head to the concrete I heard ringing in my ears so loud that I could barely make out what was going on around me. I screamed and cried in frustration from the ongoing high-pitched sound ringing loudly in my head. I wondered if I was going to have to live like that forever. I called a friend who is a nurse and asked. She said, "To be honest, we won't know. It depends on where you hit your head. Time will tell."

Everything had happened so fast that it just seemed like a nightmare. Everything felt like it was moving in slow motion. In the distance I saw my dad drop his head in his hands as he finally realized the severity of the situation and how much this damage could cost. We had to go back a short while later and look at the accident scene. Surprisingly almost nothing had happened to the car. It had a small scratch on the front bumper. But the house was in bad shape. The car had run into the first main support and completely demolished it. It had headed right toward the second one but stopped which if it had hit it, the whole house would have fallen down. It had also completely moved the stairs over.

The builder came and looked at the damage as well and said that he was glad that I had gotten out of the car because if I had stayed in it and decided to turn even a little bit from where it had ended up, the car would have hit the gas line and the whole house would have blown up. It was scary to hear that, but knowing that I made the right decision even in that scary moment was a good feeling. The other blessing was that it was the only vacant house on the block, so no one had ever lived in it.

I asked our minister to come over and bless my house to remove any of the evil feeling that I still felt lingering around me. He did and he said words that still haunt me to this day: "You are lucky and blessed that I am coming here to bless this home and not your funeral." I realized then that everything in my life and all the choices that I make are mine, and the consequences are mine too. And at the end of the day, I wasn't going to be weak. I was going to be strong. Life has its way of teaching us the lessons we need to learn. After all was said and done, that car ended up right back where it started—in the police impound and that chapter of my life was closed.

"Live as if you were to die tomorrow. Learn as if you were to live forever"

-Mahatma Gandhi

Life story by Marty Wayne Copley

My name is Marty Wayne Copley; I'm a photographer in Nashville. I've been working full time here in town for about twelve years. Before that, I was in the music industry as a writer and session player. My story of Never Giving Up took place on the fifth of February, 2016. That day, I should have been dead four times.

I was in bed and heard footsteps outside my door. I got up to see what it was. A man came in with a gun pointed at me and pulled the trigger as I stood beside my bed. For a second, I thought, am I dead? Or am I in shock? I don't feel it. I got my hand on the pistol, but I heard another click behind my head, and I got kicked. Hearing the click back, I thought, maybe it's an empty gun, because I should be dead otherwise. Who brings an empty gun to a home invasion? I don't know.

When I realized I hadn't been shot, I dropped beside my bed to get my own weapon. Because I have kids in the house, for safety, I don't keep the magazine inserted. I tried to get the magazine, but I got struck again and was pulled out into the middle of the floor. In that ordeal, I ended up with a rotator-cuff injury, so it was kind of hard to fight back at that point. But I got away from the invader briefly and stood up to charge him because I was convinced his gun was empty.

He pulled the hammer back and pulled the trigger, pushing forward again. As he did that, he pushed me into the door. That move typically means someone is expecting recoil, and if you have an empty gun, you wouldn't do that. This was the third time, but I wasn't afraid because, remember, I thought the gun was empty. We began to struggle over the weapon. He struck me in the head, and I went down. I don't know how many blows to the head I ended up with. I think there are five different spots where I've got eighteen staples keeping my head together.

I got tunnel vision and felt dizzy. I was on my hands and knees. Blood was everywhere. Head wounds bleed really badly, anyway. It was in my eyes and mouth and everything. The man shouted at me, and I realized who he was. I had been seeing someone—she was his ex-wife, but he called her his wife. We had gone to art exhibits and movies, sometimes with her daughters, who were eighteen and twenty-two. She had told me that he had some kind of medication that he had gone off and become a little more unstable. I guess he thought that if he killed me, he would get his wife and kids back.

While he was shouting and not beating me, I tried to engage him in conversation to basically get my wind back. At one point, he kind of dropped the gun to the side, away from my face. I made a fist and hit him in the groin as hard as I could. It didn't have any effect on him. He hit me again with the gun and pointed it at my face again. But it wasn't an empty gun. It was a Bersa Thunder 380, a small, compact, semiautomatic handgun. He pulled the slide back twice to clear what he thought was a jam. The second time, a live round flew. That's when I knew it was a loaded weapon. I'd more than likely be dead soon.

He kicked me in the face again and threw some expletives—you know, like, "You're going to die." I watched his finger move really slowly. It felt like it took him forever to pull the trigger. The gun was at just the right angle for me to literally look into the barrel, like in a movie or something. Have you ever had something happen in really slow motion? I mean, every detail was so vivid—what the gun looked like, what he looked like, what he smelled like. When I heard the hammer fall, nothing happened. All I could think was, Why didn't I see a flash?

I guess it was at that point, I thought I was dead. All I could think was: I wonder what it will feel like, and, my kids will never *be able to say good-bye. I won't have a face, and it'll be a closed casket. I've got 3 little boys and all I thought about was them.*

When it didn't happen, I realized I was still alive. I think the invader was in as much shock that I wasn't dead as I was. I guess the last bit of adrenaline kicked in. I open-palmed him again in the groin. I literally used his clothes to pull myself onto him, and I got him pinned to the door with my right forearm against his throat. He was still shouting about his wife and this or that. We struggled over the gun, and he hit me a few more times. I already had a black eye. He forced the gun into my mouth and pulled the hammer back, and I went to punch him. He dodged, my hand landed on the gun. Literally my thumb was toward the open end of the barrel. My little finger went between the handle and the gun itself. I knew if I could keep it there, he couldn't fire. It was down between us at one point. I thought if I could turn it toward him and pull the trigger, it should fire. I thought, I'm still alive. I don't want to kill anybody. You know these kinds of things in movies go wrong, and the wrong guy always dies.

I wanted to get the gun away from him, and I finally did. I twisted it back and threw it over my shoulder. I calmly told him, "Nobody died today. You didn't kill anybody. The gun didn't fire. If you leave now, this didn't happen." I didn't have any strength left. I bet it looked like a bad TV murder scene, with all the blood and the struggle going on. I was still really lightheaded from all the blood I had lost from the beating.

Three times, he asked for his gun back before he left. The first time I told him no and to get out. He reached over and opened the door, so I backed away and let him go. He asked for it again, and I shouted at him to leave. He was halfway down my steps. He turned around like a little kid and said, "Can I have my gun back?"

I told him, "If I find it, or better yet, if I get to mine before you're out of here, my face will be the last thing you ever see. You will leave this house in a body bag; you'll never see your kids again. Now leave!"

I stood in the window of my upstairs bedroom and gave 911 the description to the operator as he walked out into the middle of the street like nothing had happened. It was so surreal, so bizarre. He had parked his truck two streets down. He hadn't randomly passed by and decided to do something. His ex-wife had told me he had taken enough money out of their joint business account to leave the country.

I have pictures of the gun as I found it in my bedroom on the floor, fully loaded. The only thing that had saved me is that he hadn't known how to operate it. He didn't chamber the round and then pull the slide back before he came in, and that's why the first few times he pulled the handle back and pulled the trigger, nothing happened. When he thought he was clearing a jam, he was actually chambering the first round, but he did it so fast, he did two of them. The second time he pulled the trigger, that's when one flew. But that particular weapon, if you don't have the magazine completely inserted, it won't fire. I just put that to God, because there's no other reason on earth I should be here.

He got away. He was still at large three or four days later. I started posting my own homemade "wanted" posters on Facebook, showing what he looked like. I showed a picture of the gun and the bullet that was supposed to be in my head along with his face and a picture of the truck he was driving. It turns out, he had some music-industry ties as well, and we had a lot of mutual friends.

At the ER as I got stitched up, stapled up, an officer came in and asked me if I wanted to press charges. I said yes, obviously. He said, "You need to go downtown to do that when you're released from here." I signed some papers there and gave them all the information, but the police didn't seem to be that interested. While I was there, the ex-wife came to the hospital to see me with three of their kids. They kept apologizing, but all I could think of was that I was still alive. The older one said, "Why didn't you kill him? You should have killed him. You have no idea what he's done to my mother and us." But the little boy said, "I don't want my daddy to die."

In that moment I thought of my own kids. I hadn't wanted to kill him, but I probably could have. I could have gotten to my gun before he left my house. But I prayed to God. There's no other reason that I'm alive.

I was also misled about pressing charges. At the ER, I had signed some electronic pad that said I did want to, but they didn't actually file any. Almost a month later, he turned himself in, but only because his ex-wife filed domestic charges. The charges for attempted murder weren't there. The detective in the domestic-violence division was working the wife's portion of the case. I went through the roof when I found out that my charges hadn't been filed, because I was living in fear. I didn't even know that the guy was in jail, and he had turned himself in. I am a licensed carrier for my weapon, and I trained with it.

When they told me my charges had not been pressed, it was almost like the day happened all over again for me. The detective asked permission to amend the charges on my behalf. They arrested the invader, but then he was out on bond. I felt like it was never going to be over. Eventually, we did get him charged, and the DA wanted to move forward with the trial, asking for eighteen to twenty-five years. I was told that he'd probably get sentenced to twelve to fifteen years and then he'd do only five to seven. That's just how it goes. But we were going to get him. And that made me feel pretty good.

Not long after that, though, I heard through the DA's office that he had died in a car wreck.

A friend sent me a picture and asked, "Isn't this the guy that tried to kill you?" As soon as I saw his face, that fear came back, everything came back.

And I said "Yeah...but I heard that he was dead."

The unofficial story through his family was that he had heart failure and drove his car at high speed into a wall and died the next day. So, I don't know. But the bottom line is I was diagnosed with PTSD after all that. I call it hyper vigilance. Now I don't go anywhere without being armed. I just don't. I don't live in fear, but I don't think it's unreasonable to be extra prudent.

It's for nothing but the grace of God that I'm here. God saved me, absolutely. I said that from the very beginning. People say, "You've got a purpose," but I just thought it was funny. He waits until you're fifty to tell you, you have a purpose? No pressure here! Ha, ha.

Several times, I thought I was dead, three or four times, I should have been. But I never gave up. I didn't stop. Every step of the way something inside me said, "keep fighting." While he was beating me, I didn't feel the pain. I knew if I quit, if I didn't stay up on my hands and knees, if I went down, I was dead and my sons would not have me anymore. The will to survive is pretty great.

I have kids that I'm responsible for. I'm a single dad to my three boys, and it's an adventure every day. But thank God, they weren't home that day. They are the reason why I didn't give up. Thank God I didn't, because if I had, I wouldn't be here today.

http://www.martywaynephotography.com/

Chapter 14

Raise Your Words, Not Your Voice

This is probably the hardest chapter for me to write. It's tough sometimes to be this real with yourself, especially when many other people are going to read it. But since I am asking others to give me a part of themselves with their stories, I have to do the same. Things have happened in my life that affected who I am in a very personal way. I didn't ask for it, but when a person wants to take control sometimes he or she will just take it.

I was raped. Those words are hard to verbalize. It took months for me to even be able to say those words out loud without tears flowing non-stop. Still to this day I choke up when I say them, but that experience taught me a lot about my own strength and my ability to overcome fear. In the beginning after it happened I lived life as a victim. I let it hinder my ability to go out and feel comfortable in my own skin. But after counseling and talking my way through the pain I don't look at it that way anymore.

I am a **SURVIVOR** of rape. I am a strong woman and I have the power in my own life on how I choose to handle every experience that comes my way. I know that I am not alone in this experience and many women and men have struggled with this. But we can't be ashamed or afraid anymore.

Rape is considered in our society as a subject that is off topic but we can't leave it in the dark anymore. We have to let the truth come to light and give ourselves the freedom to not be afraid to speak the truth. It all begins with a conversation and being open about what has happened in our lives, good, bad, or indifferent and finding the strength and healing within each other. If you have found yourself in this position don't be afraid. Reach out if you need help or guidance and share your story so maybe you too can change the life of someone that needs it.

My life changed forever in one night. I woke up just like I had every other day, happy and enjoying the life I was living. School was out and it was summer and absolutely beautiful. My favorite time of the day in Nashville is nighttime, because the hot sun disappears but the warm weather lingers all through the night and fireflies come out and dance. This particular evening, I had gone on a walk around my neighborhood, taking in all the beauty the Nashville night had to offer. I could hear the music from the live band playing off in the distance at the marina near my house, thinking how lucky I was to be living in this incredible place. About a month before, I had met a handsome guy at the local Mexican restaurant, and he asked for my number. We started casually dating. He came over to my house a couple of times and was very polite. He was the perfect gentleman who greeted my parents and in our few times out he would always bring me home at a decent hour.

That night he asked to come over after work. Due to his respectful nature and the fact that he hadn't even tried to kiss me at that point, I agreed. Well, he didn't come to the front door as usual but the back door. I was a little confused but didn't think much of it. No sooner had I opened the door than I could tell that something was very wrong with him. His sweet and respectful ways were tainted by the strong smell of alcohol that lingered on his breath. He stumbled and pushed me across the room where my bed was. He had gotten the tour of my family home, so he knew exactly where to go. He was much bigger than me, and his muscular arms that I once thought were attractive now held me captive like a prisoner. His soft touch was now replaced with a strong aggressive grasp, and he threw me on my bed and ripped off my clothes. I wanted to scream and yell, hit him, kick him in the balls, and run. All of the things that I swore I would do if someone ever attacked me like that. Nothing came out. Not one sound. I was paralyzed, locked in fear and just prayed for it to be over. He wasn't satisfied with that, so he grabbed me and threw me into my closet. He held me hostage as silent tears fell from my eyes. I did what I could to make it stop, and then he just left me there shaking alone in the closet.

The next day, I woke up, and it was like my memory had been erased. I had been through so much trauma that my body just hid it from me like a bad game of hide and seek. I went on with my days in a normal fashion; however certain smells and clothing that I wore during the attack would set off sudden triggers. At the time I didn't even know that's what was happening. I just didn't feel right. I had angry outbursts but couldn't understand why. It wasn't until my annual doctor's appointment at the gynecologist that the horrible experience came rushing back, every last horrifying second of it. I lost all control and felt numb. I was angry, scared, confused, and embarrassed. And all I wanted was for that feeling to go away.

After that moment, I was no longer the same. My outgoing personality was replaced with a more reserved and cautious demeanor, that I still have to this day. My interest in going out to dance and move my body the way I once had was gone. The freedom of just letting my voice ring through the rafters without reservation was now caged in moments of insecurity and doubt. It's crazy how one moment can change your whole life forever. At least that's what it felt like. I learned quickly that my mind had control over my body, and even when I didn't want it to, my mind would remind me of that moment. My dad suggested that I try Qigong. I had never heard of it and had no idea what it was.

On the website from Goucher College, the term *Qigong* is made up of two Chinese words. *Qi* is pronounced "chee" and is usually translated as the life force or vital energy that flows through all things in the universe. The second word, *gong*, pronounced "gung," means accomplishment or skill cultivated through steady practice. So, Qigong also known as (Chi Kung) means "cultivating energy." It is a system practiced for health maintenance, healing, and increasing vitality.

I knew something was wrong, and I needed help, so I went to a Qigong teacher. I just didn't understand what was happening to my body and my energy. I would try to breathe deeply, but I couldn't. I would take a breath but couldn't get anything more than a shallow gasp. I grew angry with frustration because I tried over and over, wondering why I couldn't take that one deep breath that I needed and wanted so badly.

We learned through meditation and conversation that my body had gone into fight-or-flight mode. At first I didn't even realize what that meant. Fight or flight? It sounded so technical and simple. And yet I knew that what was going on with me was not simple. It affected my day-to-day life. It affected the way I slept at night, the way that I interacted with other people, and the way I felt about myself. I was a mess emotionally. But more than anything, I knew that I wanted to be okay again. I wanted the feeling of freedom, the way I knew I could be, the woman who I was before this tragic violation of trust.

Qigong was interesting because it forced my body to interact with my mind to give me the healing I desired. As I went to my sessions I could feel the old me start to come back. It's amazing how much power your mind has over your body. When I fought for that one deep breath, after a certain point, my body would just give up. It would go into flight mode, and my diaphragm would shake more vigorously the harder I tried to breathe. No matter what I did the breath would just stop, like a train coming to a screeching halt. And I would have to try again.

After months of tears, frustration, and failure, I finally overcame it. I could "Breathe Again" (a song from my favorite singer growing up, Toni Braxton. I even cut my hair short like hers...but that's another story). The hardest part of all of this was that my shallow breath affected the one thing that I loved more than anything: singing. That depth and power I had when I sang had been lessened, and my rich tone had become breathy and weak compared to what it used to be. That outside weakness also made me feel weak emotionally inside. I could see it, hear it and feel it, and that made me even more frustrated. I learned through this experience what it really meant to work.

I have done some difficult training and things in life, but this by far was the hardest thing I ever had to do. It made me face every fear I have ever had and become real with myself about what I was going through and figure out how to overcome it. I know that people look at me and my life and often make assumptions about who I am and what my life is like. But I have struggles, challenges, fears, and insecurities, just like everyone else. I just choose to take those challenges head on. I am not perfect. I am a work in progress. Through this experience I learned that it's all up to me. I choose how things are going to be in my life and I have a purpose. We all have a voice deep inside that tells us we can get through it, and we will. We just can't give up.

After this experience I have learned my own strength and my voice will no longer be silent. I will no longer be a victim of my own thoughts and insecurities. And I will never let that fight-or-flight feeling win in my life again. I want to use my words and my music to tell that story. Words are the most powerful things on this earth, so use your words with love and care, because you never know how they will affect someone else.

"Raise your words, not your voice. It is rain that grows flowers, not thunder."

-Rumi

Life story by Cynthia Tieck

I can laugh now, but it took a couple of weeks for my doctors to convince me that opioid-induced Central Nervous System Sensitization (CNSS), caused by long term use for chronic pain was the problem. By that point, I was pretty much confined to a wheelchair. I admit that I was afraid to stop the medication as it did lower my pain level for a short time.

Opioid CNSS research was so new that I basically became a test subject. Collectively, we decided the only way to prove that opioids were causing the pain was to stop taking them. I was encouraged to enter a psychiatric facility [to get off the opioids] because they had concerns that I might have seizures while stopping them. I wasn't fond of the inpatient idea because I was an opioid dependent chronic pain patient, not an addict buying street drugs to get high.

Make no mistake, opioid dependency can be just as serious as outright addiction, but the difference is I never used more than was prescribed, never used street drugs or chewed my medications to get high. I was also smart enough to know that I couldn't stop taking the opioids without medical supervision.

I began researching other options as I was not thrilled about the idea of entering an inpatient facility. What I found was shocking! The only outpatient program available in the US at that time was four states away at the Mayo Clinic and insurance wouldn't pay for the program because it included "group" therapy.

The program cost $30,000+ up front, and I would still have to pay for three weeks of transportation and lodging.

My condition continued to deteriorate rapidly and I felt like I was running out of options and definitely out of time, so I reluctantly checked myself into a local psychiatric facility. As a chronic pain patient with multiple physical issues, I was surprised to be placed in the general ward with hard core addicts—they were court ordered to be there. Twenty-four hours later, I checked myself out of the facility against advice, and became an advocate for change.

I wrote a dissertation on what needed fixing and why (my bachelor's degree was in psychology and I was working on my master's in clinical mental health when I crashed). I can happily say that the broken system was changed. Opioid dependent chronic pain patients are no longer put in with the general addict population, and the institution established outpatient programs for people like me. I actually weaned off the narcotics outpatient!

Today, I advocate not only for chronic pain patients, but also for the hard-core drug addicts who are struggling with addiction. I believe that addicts do not belong in prison unless they have committed an extremely violent crime; they need to be diverted to addiction treatment programs. These folks are not living on the streets—they are in your house! They are your children, your parents or grandparents, friends and neighbors, and they have become dependent on, or addicted to opioids. They need to be treated with dignity and compassion, not distain.

I've worked hard to change that mindset and I'm happy to say that today, there are a lot more treatment options available nationwide, including outpatient weaning programs and faith-based programs. I'm also hoping that we are making progress in changing the way we look at addicts. Minor offender addicts shouldn't be incarcerated; they need to be diverted to addiction treatment programs! Also, addiction is a family disease and needs to be treated as such.

So how did I end up in the opioid quagmire? My pain originated post surgically from a serious C-spine crush injury caused by a freak fall. Unfortunately, I'm allergic to anti-inflammatory medications (NSAIDS), and acetaminophen didn't work well, so doctors continued prescribing opioids for pain control.

A few years before the accident, I had recently returned to the United States after living overseas for several years. I spent much of my time there hiking across Europe, including the Alps. Shortly after returning, my hands swelled and became somewhat stiff. I found myself cold all the time even, though it was summer, and my hands became extremely sensitive to cold. My fingers frequently turned white and then red or blue, a phenomenon known as Raynaud's. I always had way more clothes on than my friends—even in 90-degree weather I often wore jeans and long-sleeved shirts.

About two years before the fall I was diagnosed with scleroderma, a rare autoimmune disease that hardens the skin and internal organs, causing a tremendous amount of pain and a high level of fatigue. Very little was known about the disease then and the prognosis was poor with most patients dying within five years of diagnosis. More than a quarter of all scleroderma patients spend a quarter of their lives on oxygen! With medication, I eventually recovered enough to work part time.

It's ironic that my bachelor's thesis was titled "Aging in a Youthful Society". I often joke that living with a chronic illness like scleroderma and a serious spinal cord injury gave me a crash course in the subject. You see, I was a very active individual; horseback riding, hiking, backpacking, hunting, fishing, and gardening were among my favorite activities. I spent much of my life doing environmental work.

About three weeks after the fall, I woke up on a conference trip (at the time I was co-owner of a health and safety consulting firm) and both hands and my entire chest wall were numb. I literally could not move my arms. The problem resolved, but after returning to Atlanta, I went to a neurologist and he sent me for an MRI.

I will never forget the hour he called me and said, "whatever *you do, don't fall and don't have a car wreck or you'll be a paraplegic! I want you to go home and do nothing until I can get you into surgery." That was the longest week of my life!*

A neck surgery and two knee surgeries later, I left the hospital with a long-term prescription for opioids as I was allergic to NSAIDs and the crush injury left me with a lot of pain. When I expressed concern over using them, the doctor said as he handed me the prescription, "people in pain do not become addicted to narcotics." Every doctor I saw after that for pain control issued opioids, repeating the same mantra. If only I'd known then, what we know now about opioids.

At the very least, we know that opioids can be very addicting but the long-term use of low doses of opioids can lead chronic pain patients to suffer from a more insidious problem called Central Nervous System Sensitization (CNSS) caused by the drug's ability to literally alter brain chemistry. (This is the reason why hard-core users tell us it only took using opioids for three days to lead to addiction.) For several years my pain was controlled by low doses of provider-prescribed opioids. The medication allowed me to resume many of the outdoor activities I loved.

A few years after the previous surgeries, my health began failing rapidly and I found myself in a painful downward spiral. I also broke my foot twice—and an elbow when my specialists were not conferring with each other and had me on too many CNS drugs at one time! My blood pressure dropped so low I lost muscle coordination and dropped like a rock with a 12" knife only nano inches from my nose!

I had several more surgeries, including insertion of a food tube twice from scleroderma-related complications. Life was not fun, but the opioids the doctors prescribed helped me lead a somewhat normal life. Unfortunately, over the next year, I began experiencing crazy and bizarre symptoms, including hyperreflexia, painful shooting pains, nausea, blinding headaches, and other vague and puzzling symptoms. All this led doctors to prescribe increasing doses of pain medication and other drugs to counter symptoms.

Thousands of dollars in medical tests later, doctors still could not figure out what was wrong, and many basically wrote me off as a hypochondriac. I was referred to the alternative pain-management clinic at Vanderbilt. Unfortunately, my condition continued to deteriorate.

I credit the staff at the Vanderbilt Osher Center in Nashville, Tennessee for helping me keep my sanity in an insane time! I learned meditation, tai chi, mindfulness, and had physical therapy and acupuncture (which I had to pay for as it wasn't covered by insurance.) All were helpful, but the bottom line was that my coping skills started to go as my condition continued to deteriorate further. I was quite depressed over my condition and I was losing hope, as well as function.

I developed tachycardia, even though I had no clear signs of heart disease and could no longer stand without support. I could literally feel my scalp crackling—it was the weirdest sensation and I was frightened—I didn't fear death, but I did fear living life poorly.

Then one day, my Osher counselor ran across a recently released article by Veteran's Administration (VA) doctors about a newly discovered pain syndrome, CNSS that can happen after long-term use of opioids. The VA doctors were working with veterans who were severely wounded during the Gulf War. The veterans did well on opioids for a long time, but after a few years, their pain suddenly got worse, and their physical condition rapidly deteriorated just like mine!

Puzzled, it took VA doctors several years to figure out that the only thing the veterans had in common were opioids. It was discovered that long-term use of opioids alters the brain's chemistry and causes it to send out false pain signals. The veterans were weaned off the opioids, and their pain got remarkably better.

I eventually checked myself into a local inpatient psychiatric facility, but quickly figured out they were not set up to handle chronic pain patients or disabilities. I checked myself out and wrote a dissertation on why mixing chronic pain patients in with court ordered, hard core addicts is a really bad idea!

Luckily, I had a great family support system and was able to wean off the drugs outpatient through Vanderbilt's pain management clinic. I was slowly weaned off the opioids over a six-week period. At the end of week three, I finished taking the last long-acting opioid. I woke up the next morning and thought something was wrong—until I realized that the severe pain was gone, my muscles were relaxed, and I could stand without support! I was also in very little pain.

To say I was thrilled is an understatement. Within a week, I was able to walk half a mile and I remember looking around me as I walked, thinking about how much brighter the world looked. The trees actually sparkled in the sunlight and I began a new normal. I felt like God had handed me a life line.

Outpatient weaning through a pain-management clinic is possible if you have a good support system at home. Weaning in slow, tapered doses reduces the chances of serious side effects. Are you going to feel great? No, I was fatigued and uncomfortable most of the time, but I tried to stay focused on the end goal. (However, keep in mind that depending on your personal health situation, you may need to be hospitalized for a brief period while weaning off opioids.)

Since then, I've had to have two shoulder surgeries and another neck surgery. I stopped taking the opioids as fast a possible to avoid developing CNSS again. I began educating other pain patients about the need to change the way they think about opioids and pain management, and I encourage anyone who has traveled down this road to get off the opioids but only under a doctor's care. Don't stop cold turkey; that can set off serious withdrawal symptoms that illicit drug users are so afraid of.

Opioids can insidiously change the brain chemistry in as little as three days. In talking to addicts, many have mentioned to me that they took prescription pain drugs for three days (for injuries or surgery) and knew on the fourth they didn't really need the medication but took it anyway. Most admitted they developed an overwhelming craving for the drug and the ultimate "high". Four days, that's all it took!

Frankly, I have great compassion for addicts. I know what I went through as a chronic pain patient, and because they are using much higher doses of the drugs (often chew them to get "high" quicker) and begin using more and more to get "high," they are dying at alarming rates. The road to outright addiction is much faster than most believe!

Would I ever rely so heavily on pain medication again? Never! It was a long, arduous, and very painful journey! And when I'm asked about what I do for pain, I say, "What pain?"—and really mean it. Sure, I have the aches and pains associated with aging and occasional stupidity on my part, but my life is so much better without narcotics!

For those needing surgery or experiencing painful injuries, I recommend getting off opioids as quickly as possible to avoid developing CNSS or becoming another opioid addiction statistic. You don't want to go down that very painful rabbit hole!

A few years ago, I was approached by Dr. Tracy Jackson, an associate professor of anesthesiology and pain medicine at Vanderbilt, about going public with my story. I gave a resounding "yes", and we went on television to talk about my story and the opioid crisis in this country. We also aired our mission to educate doctors and the public about CNSS.

I lobbied the state legislature and insurance companies, asking them to insure alternative pain control methods like acupuncture, mindfulness/meditation/yoga and tai chi training, to help reduce the need for opioids.

I hope by sharing my story that it will bring awareness to the fact that opioids used for more than a three days at a time, can *lead not only to addiction, but to life-altering, debilitating pain. Together Dr. Jackson and I hope to make sure CNSS does not happen to another chronic pain patient.*

To view Dr. Jackson's TED Talk on the opioid crisis, visit:
https://www.reliefretreats.com/

Raise Your Words, Not Your Voice

Chapter 15

Follow Your Passion

I get chills whenever I sing a song that touches close to my heart. I feel my tears well up as I sing. And my soul seems to just cry out with passion. I can't explain why it happens, but it's like being wrapped up in your favorite blanket or smelling your mother's homemade cookies. The familiarity and comfort that comes over you is overwhelming. It's like knowing you're doing exactly what God put you on this earth to do. And there's nothing you can do except live in that moment.

I knew from a young age that I wanted to be a singer. My mom says that when I was nine years old, I told her that, "Music is my life." And I have lived by that. I believe that as children, we know what we want to do with our lives, but oftentimes, parents and other people deter us from the path that our heart wants to take us on. They tell us, "You aren't talented enough," or "It costs too much," or, "You will never accomplish that; that doesn't happen for people like us," or whatever other negative things they can say to make you question who you are and what you want to be. I have heard that same sad story over and over again, which breaks my heart. Everyone deserves the chance to be whatever they want to be.

But the reality is that even as you grow up and take different paths, your heart never forgets. Never! You may grow up and end up going in a different direction, but the dream you have as a child will forever be a part of you. I was blessed because when I came to my mom with my dream, she already knew how I felt. She had seen it in me from when I was a baby.

In fact, as I grew up she and my dad helped in every way possible. I started my first voice lesson at five years old and soon made my first stage appearance, singing the song "Part of Your World" from *The Little Mermaid*. I can remember that moment like it was yesterday. I stepped out on that stage in front of a room full of people in my Little Mermaid outfit with a stuffed Flounder and Sebastian by my side, as the crowd eagerly waited. When I think of it now, I can still feel that wave of excitement and nervousness, confidence and fear, insecurity and passion, all in that one, single moment. It was the most amazing feeling I had ever felt, and I loved it. I was hooked. I knew that I would never give up on music, no matter what. It was a part of me. Even now when I get on stage, I feel the same thing every time. It's a high I can't explain, and it's a feeling that you don't want to end.

I started my professional career at age fourteen. I co-wrote a song called "My Heart Is Here" with a famous local DJ in the Bay Area by the name of Slammin' Sam. He had suggested that we work together, and I couldn't wait. At this point, I had only sung cover songs by famous bands or singers. But now I was going to be creating my own songs. And that lit a fire in me that was completely different. As we sat in front of the keyboard, the notes poured out and the melody and the idea began to take shape. It was like creating a really yummy cake filled with layers that were so different yet fit perfectly together. As the song progressed, each layer, piece by piece, created a different sound and emotion. The beat would bump, and eventually, it felt like your heart was moving in time to the rhythm. Then, as the keyboard played the melody lines, the smooth and melodic tones would melt your heart. To spice it up, the synthesizers would take your ears on a whole other journey, and as the sounds all melded it created the perfect combination for the finishing touch - the lyrics.

When we created "My Heart Is Here," we had no idea it would catch on so quickly. People were buying it from California to New York and all across the world. I was doing local and national interviews, and my song was placing in the top ten in DJ record pools all over. I had my song reviewed in huge dance magazines and started making a name for myself. I was so young, and the song caught a lot of attention since most of the artists in the dance market were much older than I was. I performed with my three dancers at different types of events and learned what it truly meant to be an artist. I learned how much hard work and dedication and endless sacrifice it took to accomplish this dream. And I was up for the challenge.

I started my own record label and publishing company and started learning not only the music side of the industry but the business side too, which is just as important. I remember the first time that I heard my song play on the radio. It was the most incredible feeling. It played on Wild 94.9 in San Francisco, CA which was a huge radio station where I was from. Immediately people started recognizing my music and talent, and my life was no longer the same.

Music has always had a place in my life and gotten me through all types of moments, from the saddest—like when I learned my grandfather had passed away, and I was haunted by the lyrics from The Judds song "Grandpa Tell Me 'Bout the Good Old Days," to some of the happiest, at five years old, I witnessed the emotion a song could bring as a bride sang "Wind Beneath My Wings" to her father on her wedding day. When I sang "Oh Happy Day" at my church, I felt the Lord speak to me. I listened to "Unbreak My Heart" when my high-school relationship fell apart, and sang "Como la Flor" to honor the late Selena Quintanilla, the queen of Tejano music; who is one of my idols. The song "I'm Gonna Love You Through It" helped me when my mom was diagnosed with skin cancer. And, of course, there's my favorite song of all time, "I Will Always Love You," written by the iconic Dolly Parton and sung by Whitney Houston. Music does that for all of us. We all have a memory attached to a song. Without music, we would be lost. It's everywhere we go. Music is the soundtrack of life.

"Follow your passion and success will follow you"

-unknown

Life story by Jason Cerda

My name is Jason Cerda. I started dancing when I was about five years old. What was unique about my situation was that when I started out, there weren't really any dance studios that offered hip-hop. They offered jazz, tap, and ballet, but not hip hop. I pretty much had to learn on my own—or wait till Michael Jackson or Usher or one of those guys performed on TV so I could watch. I taught myself by watching them.

Fast-forward a couple years: I entered a talent show when I was eleven, planning to dance in it, but a woman came in and asked, "Can anybody here sing? We need a singer for the talent show." Me, being a jokester, I raised my hand. I don't know for what reason, because I didn't know that I could sing at that point. She was like, "Okay, you're going to sing for the talent show."

I actually ended up singing "All My Life" by KC and JoJo—and I won. It was kind of by accident, but this started my whole fever of wanting to be an entertainer. I signed up for every talent show I could, and more often than not, I placed in the top three—or won the entire show.

In high school, I had to make a big decision. I had been a big jock my whole life, playing sports growing up. I was the captain of my football and soccer team going into high school. Senior year is the most important for a high-school athlete because that's when scouts come to look at you and decide if you are good enough to play in college. I had a couple of scouts looking at me for college soccer, but at the same time I had been offered a scholarship to a *very prestigious dance academy that had seen me in a talent show. I had to decide whether I was going to dance full time my senior year or play soccer and football.*

I danced in my senior year of high school. I also took a risk and accepted the guaranteed free education to dance, but after college I wouldn't have any guarantees. I took a lot of heat from my coaches and my teammates because I chose to dance instead of play sports. This was also back in 2005, when dancing wasn't as cool to do as it is now. It was still very underground, and it came with a lot of misconceptions.

When I graduated from college, the founder of the group NSYNC was looking to put together another boy band. I auditioned for that but didn't get it. However, an agent there was looking for people to be models and actors. He saw me and asked if I would ever consider that. I said yes, sure, I would try it out. So I ended up moving to Nashville for a year. I did a bunch of acting and modeling. Up to that point, though, I had never really recorded my singing, but I always had that idea in the back of my mind.

I don't remember how, but I met a guy down in Nashville who had a studio in his house. He said to come over, so I went. It was the first time I'd ever heard my voice on a recording. That's honestly when I got addicted. I was like, "This is what I want to do. I don't want to act. I don't want to model. I want to record music." I moved back to Virginia and started recording.

That's when Myspace was really big. I started hitting up different producers on Myspace, and I met this guy named Max Methods. He was the first producer that I worked with. He was super talented, and he produced a song that I still perform to this day called "Echate Pa'qui." The guy produced a bunch of records for me that pretty much opened my eyes to a lot of different avenues of music, like EDM, R&B and pop. The rest is history.

I put my first official song out when I was eighteen. Now I'm twenty-nine and have recorded close to a hundred songs. Some of them will never come out. Some of them are just for fun, and projects of mine. I was in the English-language market for eight years because Usher and Michael Jackson were big influences of mine growing up, but in the last four years, I have transitioned into the Latin Market. That's where I have really blossomed as an artist. I have grown a lot and found my sound.

Some of my early career highlights were opening for T. I. and T-Pain, probably one of the bigger shows I did in the English-language market. I've done shows with Ne-Yo. I've opened up for Pitbull and Jay-Z and a lot of other big-name artists even though I'm an unsigned artist.

Crossing over to the Latin side is when I got what you call "fame and success." I've been to the Grammys twice. I've been to a lot of the award shows like Premio Lo Nuestro and Premios Juventud. I've also been on TV shows that I used to watch growing up, like Despierta America and Un Nuevo Dia, which is like the Good Morning America of the Latin industry. I have also had some amazing experiences such as performing at the Puerto Rican Day Parade and People Espanol Festival in New York, Fiesta DC in Washington DC and the world famous Calle Ocho Festival in Miami. I got voted as one of the top five artists to look out for by Billboard, which was pretty cool. I also was sponsored by Subway as a Fresh Artist (Artist Fresco.) I won a contest that Univision does called Uforia Music Festival in L.A., and Subway sponsored me to come out and perform. I got to perform with big artists like J Balvin, Becky G, Nelly, and Pink. It was a cool concert, because it was Anglo and Latin artists, hip-hop artists, Mexican artists, Tejano artists, and then Camila. Plus, it had a lot of people who are really popular.

I have had three singles. My first three songs in the Latin industry have all been top twenty on the Billboard charts, and one of them actually broke top ten. My last single went number nine on the Billboard charts. I am super proud of it because I did it independently. It was pretty cool I got to see my name on the Billboard chart with a bunch of superstars signed to major labels. I was the only independent artist among all of them.

It's been a long journey because I didn't have anybody to guide me along the way. I didn't have anybody to tell me yes or no. I kind of had to do it on my own and learn by making mistakes. It's a good thing, because now that I'm really close to getting over the hump and transitioning from an independent artist into a major artist, I know what to expect, and I know what I want and what I don't want—as opposed to a lot of independent artists that are pretty naïve and will say yes to anything just for exposure.

I didn't think that I would be where I'm at right now, to be honest with you, because I started out like any eighteen-year-old with a passion for music. I never thought that I would walk into a Chipotle or to a mall or something, and people would come up to me and say, "Oh my God, I love your song! I heard it on the radio." That part of it is really cool.

A lot of times, especially early in my career when I was just trying to establish a name for myself I would do shows for free. I would drive three, four, or five hours to do a ten-minute set. In 2008, I did 150 shows. That's a lot for an independent. And all I had was my friends to help me out. I didn't have a manager or anything. It was like, "You need somebody to perform? Cool, I'll be there."

The biggest obstacle is getting people to believe in what you're doing and convincing them that it is not a hobby, that it's something you take seriously. "Okay, you want to be a doctor. Well, I want to be a singer." A lot of the general public, when they see Beyoncé on TV, they think that she just woke up like that one day. No. It was a journey for her as much as it is for anybody.

There are a lot of obstacles that any artist has to overcome. It's never easy for anyone in the music industry. There is no handbook. If you want to be a lawyer, you know you have to go to law school and pass the bar exam. If you want to become a doctor, you go to medical school. But when you want to be in the music industry, there's no school that you can go to and get a degree to be an artist and everyone follows you and pays you thousands of dollars to come perform. That's not how it works. And the music industry has changed so much. Now, with social media, it's honestly a lot harder, believe it or not, because people's attention span is super short. They want stuff instantly. Before, you only had to come out with one album a year. But now, because of Apple Music and Spotify, songs get old really, really fast, and artists are coming out with two albums a year now just to keep people happy.

It's a lot of stress on our end, and then on top of that, if you're not producing the numbers that the label wants, they drop you and take whoever's hot. Because of social media, including Instagram, there are a lot more one-hit wonders, because in the label's eyes, it can cash in on something instantly—like all these dance crazes like "Watch Me (Whip/Nae Nae),"

There's a lot less quality music coming out. But then there are artists like Bruno Mars. It took him four years to make an album. He said, "You can't rush good music. People are just putting stuff out just to put stuff out, but I can't just put out content just because, because then it tarnishes everything that I worked for."

It's a lot harder to get signed nowadays. Labels used to take a lot more chances. They used to invest a million dollars to build up an artist and make them what they wanted them to be. Now, labels are not investing. They want you to make your own brand and make yourself famous, and then all they have to do is come in and throw in a little bit of money to blow it up. Yes, having a large social media following is important. But at the end of the day you have to have a hit record. But it's not just that anymore. If you do have a hit record, do you have the image to go with it? Do you have the following on social media of "Superfans" defined as people that are willing to invest in you and your brand? Labels don't want to put any money behind marketing anymore. They just want to put out what they already know a lot of people are going to buy.

Getting signed is the struggle that I'm going through right now. Labels ask, "Well, how many followers do you have?" That's a tough question. I may have only one hundred thousand followers now, but if they got behind me, that number would quadruple, and we would both be making a lot of money. It's a struggle for a lot of artists. There are so many people I've met that you will never ever get to hear, and that is a shame. But you will never hear them because they don't have a budget to get over the hump, or they just don't have a following even though they might be super talented.

Now I have been at it for twelve years, and I've seen a lot of people stop along the way to their dreams. I've seen them all fall one by one. I'm one of the few who are still going, and at this point there's no turning back. I'm committed to it and so far invested that there's no way that I could just stop and get a nine-to-five tomorrow. It's a good and a bad thing, but I'm just determined. I don't like hearing no.

One of my biggest motivations is when I see artists on TV that I know I can compete with if given the chance. At the Grammys, I saw that stuff firsthand. I'm like, "I could be there on that stage. There's no reason I shouldn't be." When I see that, it's honestly what keeps me going. If I try and it doesn't work out, then I can at least say I had the opportunity. Until I get it, I'm going to keep going.

We are all different, but if I had to give a generic piece of advice, it would be: figure out who you want to be and put together a game plan for it. A lot of artists make the mistake of just going with the flow. They think, "Today, pop music is popular, but tomorrow, rap will be, so I'm just going to go with that too." Stay true to who you want to be and you will be appreciated a lot more that way.

And be persistent. Continue to make music and connections. I have a habit: to every person I meet, I introduce myself. I say, "Hi, I'm Jason, and I'm a singer." You never know who you're going to meet. Some have said, "You're a singer? Oh, cool. Jay-Z is my cousin." Work on your craft every single day, whether it's writing or producing or whatever it is. You can get better. I'm not the same artist that I was even three months ago. I've been working on this EP, and I didn't even know I could do something like that. I've also learned for every no that you get, there are three more yeses that you can get. So keep working until you get someone to tell you yes. You will hear no a lot, so when you get that yes, it's so satisfying.

If you have a dream, whether it's music related or not—to be a teacher, lawyer, doctor, or singer, whatever it is—follow it. Don't let other people discourage you. Be a leader and don't allow yourself to become a follower. Be someone that people admire and aspire to be. And never give up.

My motto is, follow your passion, and it will lead you to your destiny.

I am also really happy that I have gotten to turn one of my passions and goals into a reality! I've wanted to open my own dance studio for as long as I can remember and now I'm finally able to share my dream with all of you! CERDAFIED DANCE STUDIOS!!!

http://www.cerdafiedstudios.com

As written on his website Jason Cerda defines a new, multicultural era of music. Jason Cerda is the definition of a new multicultural era of music. His fusion of Pop and different genres of Latin music has left every one of his fans anticipating his newest singles. A native of Washington D.C., Cerda combines his Puerto Rican and Dominican roots with today's popular beats to take over the new Latin Urban and Tropical genres. However, he's not just known for his amazing vocals. His high-energy shows and gravity-defying choreography have made him one of the most memorable performers to come from the DC metropolitan area.

Billboard, one of the music industry's most prestigious publications, highlighted Jason Cerda as one of the top 5 new artists to lookout for in 2015. With Billboard Top 20 charting singles Al Lado Mio, Color Favorito, and Un Poco Mas under his belt, Cerda has successfully toured in the US, Dominican Republic, Colombia, Puerto Rico, and Guatemala building fan bases all over Latin and Central America. Most recently, he has won over Colombia's heart with his performances at the Latino Show Awards in Medellin and a high-end fashion show soon after. Jason's charm won him the public's popular vote when he was selected to perform at one of the country's biggest summer concerts, the 2014 Uforia Music Festival in Los Angeles.

Cerda has also performed at other key and notable events in the Hispanic community such as the Puerto Rican Day Parade and People Español Festival in New York, Fiesta DC in Washington DC, the world-famous Calle Ocho Festival in Miami, and Calibash Music

Festival in Las Vegas, NV. Singing and writing in both English and Spanish has given him the ability to reach a wide fan-base all over the world. Cerda's beautiful smile and charming eyes have not gone unnoticed either giving him the title of one of DC's sexiest bachelors by Inside Edition. Deriving from his Latino heritage and deep admiration for Michael Jackson, Cerda fuses Pop and R&B melodies with Latin beats. Cerda's latest single, Telefone, was an international phenomenon since its release in January 2018, charting in France, Colombia, Peru, and Canada

Jason Cerda's music is available for digital download where all music is sold and all social media can be found at:

http://www.jasoncerdamusic.com/

Never Give Up

Never Give Up! What's amazing is that each word has its own individual power. Together the words *never give up* represent the most powerful and life-affirming choice that you can make.

Never - when you hear this word, it resonates with resolution. We associate it with something that will no longer happen again—something that we will no longer tolerate or accept.

Give - there is no more beautiful, passionate, and caring word than that. It is an unselfish word that we use to show our affection and love toward others. It is an act of doing something for someone else or even for ourselves.

Up - it makes you feel something positive, uplifting, and inspired.

All of us, whether we have said those words to ourselves silently in the backs of our minds or read them on a poster or heard someone chanting them in the background, have been exposed to it our whole lives.

We face the reality of where life has taken us every day. Whatever the pain or lesson may have been, something had to change. Life came to a pivotal moment when you said, "I am no longer going to think this way, feel this way, act this way, treat others this way, or live my life this way." It is in this single moment that life changes. And all of those things that challenged you, force you to fight for a better life.

We all have trials and tribulations. All of us! We all have these moments in different capacities. We all know what it feels like to go through things that make us weak and challenge our own capabilities. But that's what makes us human. That's what makes us vulnerable, capable, driven, and fearful—and able to relate to one another if we just take the time.

More than anything what I want people to get from this book is that we are all in this life together. We are all moving and living and breathing at the same time. Everyone on earth gets twenty-four hours a day and it's up to us how we use each hour, each minute, and second. It's up to us to take care of one another and to know that we aren't alone in this life, even though at times it can feel lonely. We owe it to ourselves to learn everything we can from one another in this crazy, wonderful journey we call life. And no matter what we experience, good or bad, we need to continue to grow and learn.

Know that you are not alone as you face each new challenge in your life. God is watching over you and He loves you. You have the power to get through anything in this life. Just believe in yourself, find your warrior within, and never give up!

Acknowledgements

First and foremost, I want to thank God our Heavenly Father, because without His love and guidance, I would not be here on this earth. I thank my mom and dad for giving me life and also for sacrificing everything they had to let me follow my dreams. And I want to thank my sweet daughter Isabella, for just being you. You have inspired my life and my heart in a whole new way and shown me what unconditional love means. I promise to always love you and take care of you my sweet little princess.

I also want to thank everyone who contributed their stories to this book. You are all warriors. It means so much to me that you took the time to write your story or let me interview you and get a glimpse into your amazing and inspirational lives. Every one of you is so special, and I know that your story will help motivate and change the lives of those who read this book.

Manuel Pena, I have known you a long time. In fact, we were kids when we met. I know that many of your decisions have greatly affected your life, but learning about your struggle and what you have been through, I am so proud of the man that you have grown up to be. I know that one day, as that dark chapter of your life ends, you will use that experience to help change other people's lives as well as your own. You will achieve all the dreams that you set out to follow and not repeat your past choices. Never give up, Manuel.

Mignon Francois, it was such an honor hearing you speak at the small-business expo where we met. When I asked to interview you for my book, you smiled and welcomed me with open arms without hesitation. It was also an honor getting to sit one-on-one with you and learn about who you are and what you have accomplished. You are such an incredible role model, and you have accomplished so many things in the face of adversity.

Karen Mock, my wonderful Aunt Karen, you are such an incredible woman, and hearing what you have overcome to be where you are in life has been amazing. You fought your addiction with such strength and faith. God will always remember that. Even when things were tough, you found Him and reached out, and He answered and healed you. Your talent in your doodles and the way you inspire others through your art and message are wonderful. It is amazing, the way that you create without boundaries and are able to express emotion without words, just colors and shapes. Love you!

Linda and John Martinez, mom, dad I love you both so much! You are my parents, my role models, and my best friends. And I thank you for everything you have done in my life.

T. J. Cates, I am so proud of what you and Jill are accomplishing and how you are growing your vision. Just since our interview, you have expanded and become even more successful. Your drive to help young talent and to help artists grow in their careers and vision is wonderful, and I am so excited to see what the future brings to *Nashville Entertainment Weekly*.

Joanna Vasquez, I am so thankful for your friendship after all these years. We are all so blessed to know you and happy that you are here to share your amazing life with your husband and your sweet little angel and to tell your story of beating the odds. We have known each other for so long; to see and know that now, you are on the incredible journey of motherhood is such a blessing. You are a great mother and so beautiful inside and out.

Marty Wayne Copley, you are a fighter in all senses of the word. I am so blessed that you were able to share your story. In the short amount of time I got to sit with you, I learned what an incredible passion you have for your children, photography, people in general, and your role model and best friend, your father. God bless his soul. I know that what you went through was tough, and I thank you for sharing your story.

Jayce Hein, it was such a pleasure to interview you and hear your story. I am so inspired by you. Your talent of writing hit songs and then the ability to conquer such an incredible goal is extraordinary. Many people have goals they say they want to reach, but then they just give up. You didn't. You lived in that moment in every way until you succeeded in accomplishing all of your dreams.

Erion Moore II, the moment that I met you your personality was larger than life, and I knew right away we would be good friends. You have defied the odds and have survived when others have not. You are truly a miracle and inspiration.

Jerrod Kerr, you are a champion, plain and simple. The way you think and the way that you approach what has happened in your life is so amazing! Where most people would fall apart, you became stronger and not only inspired yourself but those around you. And that is what defines a true *hero*!

Ricky Mena, you are such an amazing human being. I am so honored to know you and call you a friend. The impact that you have on so many children's lives and their families, all over the country and now the world, is incredible. I know God is working through you in so many ways, and having that inspiration come from your grandmother is just a reaffirmation that you are doing exactly what you were put on this earth to do. I know that as you continue to grow your foundation, Heart of a Hero, more and more people will be inspired to help make a difference.

Paula Smith, you are such a sweet and incredible soul, and I know that sharing your story took a lot for you to do. But I am so thankful that you did. You are such a strong and powerful woman, and I am so glad that now the world can see what I see. You are such a great friend, and I know that God has so many more blessings for you.

Jax Young, thank you so much for sharing your story. You are an incredible role model and possess such a great talent. Your strength, humility, and determination to make a difference to our Veterans and to the world is so inspiring. I pray that this book helps to get your message out that we need to give Veterans "A Help Up, Not A Hand Out." God has many great things planned for you and your charity. Thank you most of all for your service to this country. You are a soldier in every sense of the word and we are so lucky to be protected by people like you that sacrifice everything to allow us to live safe, happy and free.

Ana Maria Castaneda, sweetie, you have such an amazing heart. I am so thankful that you took the time to write your story and also let me spend time with you and Luca as we began working on your story for this book. You have overcome so much in your life, and I appreciate you sharing your journey. It's so interesting, because now I am exactly where you were when we did our interview. So, maybe out of everyone, I was the one that needed to hear it the most. God was setting the stage for me to understand what this next step in my life would be. You are an incredible mother, and Luca is very lucky to have you.

Cynthia Tieck, you are my second mom and one of my best friends, and I am so thankful that I have you in my life. If I have a question about anything, I know that you will have an answer for me. You have such an amazing spirit, and no matter what life throws at you, you always kick it right in the a**. And I love that! You are so caring toward others and do your best to make sure that you educate people and give them all the information they need to have successful and healthy lives.

Jason Cerda, I am so excited that you are a part of this book. I have seen your talent just grow and grow and grow. I was there when you had just decided that being a recording artist was the dream that you were going to follow. It has been such a blessing to watch all the hard work that you have put in pay off. And to see the dream you have of your own dance studio come into existence. You deserve all of it. I am so proud of you.

Thank you, Sam Rockford, for transcribing these interviews for me. You always do such a great job, and you always got them back to me right when I needed them. And thanks to James for recommending you. Also thank you to my awesome attorney A.J. Arias who has given me great legal guidance and support.

And thanks to my amazing friend who created the artwork for this book, KyroWolf—whom I call family. You are so incredibly talented, and every time I see your work, it just blows me away. Not only are you the most talented graphic artist that I know, you have the greatest heart and are so kind and supportive. You have always believed in my music and my dreams since the day we met, and I am forever thankful for your friendship and your incredible talent.

I also want to thank everyone who has played any part in my life in regard to music, friendship, or just being a great support or role model. You mean the world to me. Without all of you, this book would not have been possible. You all have inspired me, motivated me, and believed in me, and that means everything.

And most of all I want to thank you for reading this book. You are helping me live my dream of being an author. I hope as you have read each chapter that this book has inspired you, and motivated you. I hope it has made you laugh and cry and touched your heart the same way it has mine. I hope it has made you believe that you can conquer anything that is put in front of you no matter how hard it feels and that you are not alone in your trials and tribulations. You have a warrior within you and with faith, love and determination you will be able to overcome anything. Never Give Up!

Resources

Addiction definition, Dictionary.com 2018

https://www.dictionary.com/browse/addiction

Skin Cancer Foundation. "Skin Cancer Facts and Statistics." The Skin Cancer Foundation

https://www.skincancer.org/skin-cancer-information/skin-cancer-facts

Cancer.org. "Cancer Fact and Figures 2018." American Cancer Society, 2018

https://www.cancer.org/research/cancer-facts-statistics/all-cancer-facts-figures/cancer-facts-figures-2019.html

McGrew, Phil. "Defining Your External Factors." Dr.Phil.com, Sept. 5, 2002

https://www.drphil.com/advice/defining-your-external-factors/

Scleroderma Foundation, "What is scleroderma." Scleroderma Foundation 2018

https://www.scleroderma.org

National Heart, Lung, and Blood Institute. "How The Lungs Work." *U.S. Department of Health and Human Services*

https://www.nhlbi.nih.gov/health-topics/how-lungs-work

The 5 Love Languages. "Discover Your Love Language." Northfield Publishing and Moody Publishers, 2019

https://www.5lovelanguages.com/

Goucher College. "Stress Management." *Yoga, Meditation and Self Care,* 2018

https://www.goucher.edu/learn/academic-support-and-resources/ace/stress-management

Quotes

"No matter how hard the past has been you can always begin again"

Buddha

https://tinybuddha.com/quotes/june-15-2010/

"Limits, like fear, are often an illusion"
Michael Jordan
https://www.inspiredtoreality.com/pin/limits-like-fears-are-often-just-an-illusion/

"Courage is knowing what not to fear"
Plato
https://www.brainyquote.com/quotes/plato_104744

"Life Begins When Addiction Ends"

https://www.pinterest.com/pin/398498267011363340/

"Cancer does not have a face until it's yours or someone you know"
https://twitter.com/nfcr/status/968125592494313473

"Turn your wounds into wisdom"
Oprah
https://www.thefreshquotes.com/oprah-winfrey/

"Live as if you were to die tomorrow. Learn as if you were to live forever"
Mahatma Ghandi
https://www.brainyquote.com/quotes/mahatma_gandhi_133995

"Be kind, for everyone you meet is fighting a hard battle"
Plato
https://www.passiton.com/inspirational-quotes/5041-be-kind-for-everyone-you-m-

"Life is 10% what happens to you and 90% how you react to it"
Charles Swindoll
https://quotefancy.com/quote/50339/Charles-R-Swindoll-Life-is-10-what-happens-to-you-and-90-how-you-react-to-it

"The race of life is a marathon, not a sprint"
Tony Robbins
https://quotefancy.com/quote/923152/Tony-Robbins-The-race-of-life-is-a-marathon-not-a-sprint

"If you dream it, you can do it"
Walt Disney

https://womeninspiring.com/2017/05/if-you-can-dream-it-you-can-do-it/

"There are 86,400 seconds in a day. It's up to you to decide what to do with them."
Jim Valvano
https://www.azquotes.com/quote/562476

"Love Always Finds a Way"
Guy Finley
https://www.facebook.com/guyfinleyofficial/photos/love-always-finds-a-way-guy-finley-inspirationalquotes-love-wisewednesday-lettin/10160623537535634/

"Raise Your words, not your voice. It is rain that grows flowers, not thunder"
Rumi
https://quotefancy.com/quote/3833/Rumi-Raise-your-words-not-voice-It-is-rain-that-grows-flowers-not-thunder

"Follow Your Passion and Success Will Follow You"

http://www.passionpluspurpose.com/2016/03/06/follow-your-passion-and-success-will-follow-you/

About the Author

Photography by Joshua Johnson

Angela Martinez was born and raised in California. Her passion and love for music was the inspiration for her move to Nashville. While pursuing her music career, she completed her education from Middle Tennessee State University with a Bachelor of Liberal Studies (BLS) degree. She is a member of Sigma Alpha Lambda, a National Leadership and Honors Organization, Nashville Area Hispanic Chamber of Commerce where she is in charge of membership, Latinos for Tennessee, and P.E.O. a philanthropic education organization that helps empower women through educational scholarships, grants, and loans for college. She is also the mentorship coordinator for Men of Valor.

Angela resides in Nashville, Tennessee and spends her time singing, writing songs, and spending time with her beautiful daughter Isabella.

Currently she is writing her new book "Warrior Within" and will be releasing her single "Warrior Within" in the upcoming year.